TRAGEDY AT TAOS:

THE REVOLT OF 1847

Charles Bent
first American governor of New Mexico.

(From *The History of the Military Occupation of the
Territory of New Mexico from 1846 to 1851 by the
Government of the United States,*
by Ralph Emerson Twitchell.)

TRAGEDY AT TAOS:

THE REVOLT OF 1847

James A. Crutchfield

Republic of Texas Press

Library of Congress Cataloging-in-Publication Data

Crutchfield, James Andrew, 1938-.
    Tragedy at Taos : the revolt of 1847 / by James A. Crutchfield.
        p.   cm.
    Includes bibliographical references and index.
    ISBN 1-55622-385-4
    1. Mexican War, 1846-1848—New Mexico.   2. New Mexico—History—
    To 1848.   3. Bent, Charles, 1799-1847—Assassination.   I. Title.
    E405.2.C85   1995
    973.6'23—dc20   94-49513
                                                                 CIP

ISBN 1-55622-385-4
10 9 8 7 6 5 4 3 2 1
9501

All inquiries for volume purchases of this book should be addressed to
Wordware Publishing, Inc., at 1506 Capital Avenue, Plano, Texas 75074.
Telephone inquiries may be made by calling:

(214) 423-0090

"...the conspirators had their plans laid to bring about a general uprising of Mexicans and Indians in New Mexico, and they evidently thought with this combination of forces, they would be able to drive the Americans out of the territory, and keep them out."

Dick Wootton, quoted from *"Uncle Dick" Wootton*, by Howard Lewis Conard, 1890.

"In New Mexico everything was in a peaceful, prosperous condition, to all outward show; the people traded freely; small foraging and herding parties of American soldiery were everywhere scattered, placing confidence in the inhabitants. It was afterward seen that designing men—artful and learned natives— were busy, insidiously sowing the seeds of discontent among the more ignorant class of the community, more especially the Pueblo Indians. The result was, they soon considered themselves outraged—their lives at stake—their possessions in danger. With inflamed passions, perverted minds, the brutal attack upon Governor Bent was commenced...."

Lewis Hector Garrard, from his book, *Wah-To-Yah and the Taos Trail*, 1850.

FOR MY WIFE, REGENA

Contents

Contents

Illustrations

Introduction

During the early morning hours of January 19, 1847, the newly appointed American governor of the territory of New Mexico, Charles Bent, was savagely murdered in his home in the small village of Taos. The perpetrators of the heinous crime were Mexican and Indian malcontents from the town and from the nearby Taos Pueblo. Still smarting over the recent American occupation of this one-time part of Mexico, the crowd continued its bloodbath until five more leading New Mexican citizens were murdered and mutilated.

A couple of weeks later, in a battle that lasted for the better part of two days, volunteer and regular elements of an American army bombarded the dissidents at their refuge in Taos Pueblo and subdued them. The instigators of the earlier Taos murders were arrested, tried, and within weeks, hanged for their crimes.

In the pages that follow, the events of January 19, 1847 have been recalled, as well as those of the weeks immediately before and after the murders in Taos. Background material about the times surrounding the incident has also been presented to suggest to the reader that the killings were not merely isolated events in a remote Southwestern town. Indeed, the episode represented an important milestone in the establishment of the American presence in New Mexico.

The Taos Revolt has intrigued me for years, and I have written several magazine articles about the episode. But, in my research for those articles, I quickly discovered that there were no full-length books, at least that I could find, that gave the complete history of the incident and the events leading up to it. Michael McNierney's book *Taos 1847: The Revolt in Contemporary Accounts*, as the title indicates, contains several renditions of the revolt and its aftermath by eyewitnesses and those who arrived at the scene soon afterwards. And, I also found references to the incident in several old histories and recollections of the Mexican War, written by men who took part in the action themselves. Furthermore, from a modern standpoint, there are intriguing chapters about the uprising in Bernard DeVoto's *The Year of Decision: 1846*, in David Lavender's *Bent's Fort*, and in Paul Horgan's *Great River: The Rio Grande in North American History*. Otherwise, however, there just does not appear to be a great deal of written material about this extremely important episode in the history of the Southwest.

I hope this book will partially fill the vacuum in the literature concerning the Taos Revolt of 1847. Using accounts extracted from government documents, personal diaries, and writings of eyewitnesses, I have attempted to analyze the events of late 1846 and early 1847, as they occurred in the remoteness of northern New Mexico, in a manner and with a perspective that will allow the modern reader to judge for himself the relevance of this century-and-a-half-old uprising.

I would be quick to point out that this book is a glimpse of the Taos Revolt from the American viewpoint only. Every event that has ever occurred in the history of the world has had at least two, and sometimes many more, versions of its cause and outcome. Wartime issues seem to be especially subject to multiple interpretations, depending upon whether one is on the winning or losing side. In addition to the American view, a book is needed that explores and details the Mexican aspect of the Taos Revolt, as well.

It is often said that a writer's best friends are the works of those who wrote before him, and it is no different with the present volume. While accurate material about the Taos Revolt is admissibly sparse, I was not shy about utilizing that which was available. These titles are listed in the bibliography.

I would like to thank my wife and partner, Regena, for her support during the times that I immerse myself in writing and for her companionship when we visit some remote spot that only a rabid historian and writer could appreciate. Thanks also to Mary Bray Wheeler, who graciously took time from her own busy writing schedule to edit an earlier version of the manuscript. Any errors in the book due to interpretation of fact, however, are mine alone.

James A. Crutchfield

Franklin, Tennessee
Taos, New Mexico

THE SETTING

The circumstances which led to the brutal murder of Governor Charles Bent in Taos, New Mexico, on January 19, 1847, were rooted in distant events that occurred in the vast land known as Texas. Originally part of Mexico, and earlier still, a vital possession of Spain in the New World, Texas was a hot-bed for American revolutionaries starting in the late days of the eighteenth century.

As early as 1791, Philip Nolan, a friend and protege of General James Wilkinson, made a trip into Texas, ostensibly as a trader. Nolan, a Kentucky adventurer who had once worked as a shipping clerk for Wilkinson, lost all of his goods to Spanish authorities. However, in later years, he returned to Texas as a "mustanger," one who captured wild horses for resale. By that time, Nolan's mentor, Wilkinson, the commanding general of the United States Army, had become involved in the so-called "Spanish Conspiracy," a plot to sever the western section of the newly formed United States from the central government and to organize a separate country with strong allegiances to Spain. Teaming up with former Vice President Aaron Burr to further his scheme, Wilkinson finally turned state's evidence on Burr and escaped from the plot with his own reputation unharmed.

With Wilkinson's penchant for the clandestine, who is to know at this late date whether Philip Nolan's real purpose in traveling to Texas was not to spy out the land for his designing associate? Indeed, Nolan's close friendship with Wilkinson has led some modern-day authorities to speculate that, actually, Nolan was serving as the general's agent and that his missions were designed more around data gathering for Wilkinson's conspiratorial efforts than for capturing wild horses.

In any event, on his last trip, which occurred in 1800, Nolan, along with twenty-seven other adventurers, built a crude fort near today's Waco, where he was killed by soldiers of the Spanish militia. Several of Nolan's small army, including a Tennessee mercenary, Ellis Peter Bean, were captured by the Spanish and kept incarcerated in Mexico for years. Bean was fortunate enough to finally be released by his captors and later fought against the British in the Battle of New Orleans and lived to see the United States and Mexico declare war on one another in 1846.[1]

Some nineteen years later, Dr. James Long, a Virginian who had served as a surgeon in the War of 1812 and who, ironically, was married to General James Wilkinson's niece, attempted his own invasion of Texas. The recent announcement of the Adams-Onís Treaty between the United States and Spain had infuriated many Americans living in Louisiana and Mississippi. The treaty placed the boundary line between the U.S. and Spain along the Sabine River and thus did not include Texas as an American territory. James Long, whose residence for the past few years had been in southwestern Mississippi, assembled three hundred followers and marched into Texas, captured the town of Nacogdoches, and formed a republic with himself as president. Although attempts were made for the establishment of a legitimate government, complete with provisions for the settlement of emigrants from the United States, the Long republic was short-lived and did not survive its founder's murder in 1822. Nevertheless, Dr. Long's aborted attempt to claim independence for Texas can truly be called the first American effort at such an endeavor.[2]

> *Declaration of the independence of Texas.*
> The Louisiana Herald, contains a copy of a declaration, issued on the 23d of June, by the supreme council of the republic of Texas. The following extracts contain all that would be interesting to the American reader.
> The citizens of Texas would have proved themselves unworthy of the age in which they live—unworthy of their ancestry—of the kindred republics of the American continent—could they have hesitated in this emergency, what course to pursue. Spurning the fetters of colonial vassalage, disdaining to submit to the most atrocious despotism that ever disgraced the annals of Europe—they have resolved, under the blessing of God, to be FREE. By this magnanimous resolution, to the maintainance of which their lives and fortunes are pledged, they secure to themselves an elective and representative government, equal laws and the faithful administration of justice, the rights of conscience and religious liberty, the freedom of the press, the advantages of liberal education, and unrestricted commercial intercourse with all the world.
> "Animated by a just confidence in the goodness of their cause, and stimulated by the high object to be obtained by the contest, they have prepared themselves unshrinkingly to meet, and firmly to sustain, any conflict in which this declaration may involve them.
> "Done at Nacogdoches this twenty-third day of June, in the year of our Lord 1819.
> JAMES LONG,
> *President of the Supreme Council.*
> BIS'TE TARIN, sec'ry.

James Long's Texas Declaration of Independence

(From *Nile's Register* September 11, 1819)

In 1821, from a more peaceful standpoint, Moses Austin, a resident of Missouri, was granted a large expanse of land along the lower Colorado and Brazos rivers in today's state of

Texas. Financial troubles had driven Austin to Texas, where Spanish authorities gave him permission to settle several hundred Americans on his 200,000-acre tract. Before Austin could get underway with his colonization scheme, however, he died.

At about the same time, a far-reaching event occurred. Mexico obtained its independence from Spain and thus became the rightful owner of the land which had been granted to Austin. Stephen Austin, Moses's son, pursued the matter after his father's death. Stephen quickly persuaded the new Mexican government to allow him to inherit the elder Austin's landholdings, along with his right to settle the American families. Obtaining this approval, Stephen assumed command of the emigrant movement, thus heralding the first legitimate American settlement of Texas. Stephen's plan for an American-occupied Texas initially called for the entity to operate within the existing framework of the Mexican government, and Austin proved himself to be a patriotic Mexican subject.

Both Austin and his followers, as well as Mexican authorities, were pleased with the arrangement. Over the next few years, more grants were issued to anxious Americans who were eager to leave the East and make new beginnings for themselves beyond the Mississippi River. By 1824, when the Mexican state of "Texas y Coahuila" was organized, several thousand Americans had already firmly established themselves—some legally and some illegally—in the Brazos River valley. There was plenty of land for everyone, the Mexican government thought, and here, on the new country's northeastern frontier, the population was so sparse that it seemed better to have someone on the land—Americans or otherwise—than to leave it totally barren for the dry summer winds to blow away.[3]

In late 1826 a small army of about thirty American settlers, led by a disgruntled Mississippian, Benjamin Edwards, tried once again to establish an independent republic of Texas.

Edwards' brother Haden had acquired some 300,000 acres of land from the Mexican government the previous year, but had disregarded the rights of earlier Americans who had already staked claims in the same area.

While Haden was visiting the United States, Benjamin was confronted with the news that Mexican authorities had revoked his brother's claim and was ordering the pair out of the country. Benjamin and his thirty followers occupied Nacogdoches on December 16 and announced the "Republic of Fredonia." Plans called for Texas to be divided between the Fredonians and dissatisfied Cherokee Indians, who had recently moved into the region but who could not obtain land grants on their own from the Mexican government. However, when 250 Mexican soldiers, supported by one hundred of Stephen Austin's colonists—who didn't like the Edwards brothers' tactics any more than the Mexicans did—marched on Nacogdoches in late January, 1827, the revolution fizzled. Both of the Edwards brothers returned to the United States, leaving the original settlers of their massive claim breathing a sigh of relief.[4]

As more and more Americans became entrenched in their new Mexican homes, United States authorities attempted to acquire that northern province of Mexico known as "Texas and Coahuila." President John Quincy Adams, through his minister to Mexico, Joel Poinsett, offered one million dollars for the territory, only to be scorned by Mexican officials.

On March 4, 1829, Andrew Jackson was inaugurated as president of the United States. A product of the wild frontier himself and an acknowledged expansionist, Jackson soon made it known that "Texas and Coahuila," in which so many Americans now lived, would better be a part of the United States than of a foreign power like Mexico. In a letter dated June 8, 1829, written to John Overton, his close friend and one-time law partner back in Tennessee, Jackson declared:

> I have long since been aware of the importance of
> Texas to the United States and of the real necessity of

extending our boundary west of the Sabine.... I shall keep my eye on this object & the first propitious moment make the attempt to regain the Territory as far south & west as the great Desert.[5]

President Andrew Jackson

(From oil painting in the White House)

Later the same year, President Jackson attempted to negotiate with Mexican authorities for the purchase of the "Texas" part of the state of "Texas and Coahuila" for five million dollars. Like President Adams's proposition before him, Jackson's offer was rejected, and Mexican authorities demanded that Joel Poinsett, still the U.S. minister, be recalled. Fuming over the issue, the President referred to the dilemma in his 1829 message to Congress when he declared that the United States' position on the Texas question was to "ask for nothing that is not clearly right and to submit to nothing that is wrong." Mexican authorities viewed this high-toned conversation and Jackson's move to acquire Texas through purchase as an act of overt imperialism.

By 1830, despite the failure of President Jackson to buy the American-inhabited zone of Texas, more than thirty thousand Americans lived in the region. Mexico expressed second thoughts about its earlier generosity regarding colonists from the United States. Suddenly Americans were everywhere, and the brash invaders were not so welcome anymore. A local newspaper commented about the peculiar people from far away:

> "he [an American] is always astute and agile: his penetrating observation never deserts him, and he is quick to seize any occurrence and turn it to his advantage. Moreover, he has a thousand ways of acquiring his necessities.[6]

A contemporary Mexican observer added:

> How strange are these people from the North...! The Americans...eat only salted meat, bread made by themselves out of corn meal, coffee, and home-made cheeses. To these the greater part of those who live in the village add strong liquor, for they are in general, in my opinion, lazy people of vicious character.[7]

In 1830, after reconsidering its land grant policies to foreigners, the Mexican government closed its frontier to all newcomers, especially Americans, and made it known that no more immigrants would be accepted.

By then, however, it was too late. The floodgates in the United States were open. All across the land back East, residents were selling their farms and stores, packing up their wagons with all of their earthly possessions, and heading for the newfound land of opportunity. "GTT" signs sprang up all over the South and East, indicating that the former property owners had "Gone to Texas." Thousands of Americans were on the move, and officials in Mexico realized more and more that they had a very real problem on their hands.

Finally, in 1834, Stephen Austin presented a petition to President Santa Anna demanding that Texas be organized into a separate state, but one still under Mexican authority. Santa Anna, who had been in and out of political power for a number of years, had Austin arrested and jailed. But, while Austin brooded away in a Mexican prison, momentum was rapidly gaining for Texas independence from its mother country.

Some Texas residents were willing to use force to gain their independence. In late June, 1835, William B. Travis, a South Carolina schoolteacher and lawyer, accompanied by a few Americans, stormed the Mexican garrison at Fort Anahuac, demanding its surrender and receiving it. Then, in October of the same year, in what some historians call the first battle of the Texas Revolution, a small army of Texas settlers defeated a troop of Mexican cavalry near the Guadalupe River in central Texas.

On March 2, 1836, the Texas Declaration of Independence was unanimously approved by fifty-nine Texans who had gathered at the provisional capital at Washington-on-the-Brazos. Even as that historic meeting was being attended, Santa Anna was quickly tightening his grip on Texas forces gathered inside the Alamo at San Antonio. Since February 23, some four thousand Mexican soldiers had surrounded the old Spanish mission and watched as the small Texas army inside slowly ran out of food and water. During the dawn hours of March 6, the Mexican army made its final assault. All of the Anglo-Texan defenders inside the mission were killed, including Travis; Texas Ranger James Bowie; and the former Tennessee congressman David Crockett.[8]

Later in March, Colonel James W. Fannin, who for a brief time earlier in the year had served as commander-in-chief of the Texas army, along with three hundred Texans, were captured by forces of General José Urrea near Goliad. After two days of attempting to defend his position, Fannin's only choice became surrender. On March 27, 1836, in direct conflict to Urrea's promise of clemency for the Texans, all were massacred by order of President/General Santa Anna.[9]

Texans sprang back though. To the war cries, "Remember the Alamo" and "Remember Goliad," General Sam Houston's troops defeated Santa Anna's army at San Jacinto on April 21, thus assuring, once and for all, independence for Texas.

A degree of normalcy returned to Texas following the war for independence. Sam Houston, the former Tennessee congressman and governor, was elected the republic's first president, and Texas was formally recognized as a sovereign state by many foreign countries, including the United States. But, annexation was already being fostered by many Texans and Americans alike. It took only about ten years for the question of the permanent Texas-American relationship to gain a first-place spot on the agendas of many statesmen in both Washington and in Mexico City.

When Texas won its independence from Mexico in 1836, it defined its western border as a line running along the channel of the Rio Grande to the river's source, and from that point, a straight line due north for three hundred miles. The real estate thus contained within the Republic's borders encompassed the entire eastern half of today's state of New Mexico, including the towns of Santa Fe and Taos.

Mirabeau B. Lamar, who succeeded Sam Houston as president of Texas, took over the reins of government in 1838. He immediately set about to bring Texas into the modern age with improved roads and an expanded school system. The republic, however, was suffering from economic bad times, and within three years from the date Lamar took office, the public debt had swelled to more than seven million dollars. Yet, Texas officials continued to spend more than a million dollars a year, while the republic's annual income was less than half a million dollars.

Lamar thought that his country's economic woes could be improved if Texas established trade relations with the prosperous Santa Fe markets, which he believed to lie within his republic's boundaries. Costly Cuban merchandise could be unloaded on the Texas Gulf coast, routed through Austin, then sent directly to Santa Fe, thus saving hundreds of miles off the traditional route from Missouri to New Mexico via the Santa Fe Trail. Texas coffers would fill rapidly, according to Lamar's thinking, from providing the freighting facilities for all of this rich trade.

In 1839 Lamar urged his congress to approve an expedition to Santa Fe to explore and—he hoped—to confirm his trade theory. The issue simmered for a while, until April 1841, when the following announcement was placed by Lamar's operatives in the *Austin City Gazette*:

> Having been authorized...to organize a military force for the purpose of opening a commercial intercourse with the people of Santa Fe; for which purpose troops are necessary to escort the merchandise through the Comanche wilderness. I therefore respectfully address myself to the young men of the country.... All who arm, mount and equip themselves, will receive the pay of mounted gunmen.... Ten large road-wagons will be furnished by the

the merchants...this expedition will furnish an ample field for adventure....[10]

On June 20, 1841, between three and four hundred men and boys, along with as many horses and a score of supply wagons, left Austin on the first leg of the so-called Texan-Santa Fé Expedition. Their destination was far-off Santa Fe, and before the trip was over, the group's journey took them north out of Austin to the Chihuahua Trail, then more or less westwardly across the parched Llano Estacado to San Miguel in the eastern part of today's state of New Mexico.

But San Miguel was as far as most of the weary travelers got. The expedition, due to lack of provisions, eventually broke up into two groups in West Texas, and both elements suffered from weeks of grueling travel that quenched even the brightest fires of enthusiasm. Tired of the hunger, thirst, and threat of Indian attack, components of both parties straggled into San Miguel during the autumn days of 1841, only to

The village of San Miguel, New Mexico

(From *Report of Lieut. J.W. Abert, of his Examination of New Mexico in the Years 1846-'47*)

be arrested by waiting Mexican soldiers under the direction of Manuel Armijo, the governor of New Mexico.

The surviving members of the Texan-Santa Fé Expedition were then marched, under armed guard, all the way to Mexico City. George Wilkins Kendall, a newspaperman who had participated in the expedition and was one of the captives, wrote of the departure in his book *Narrative of the Texan Santa Fé Expedition*:

> After we had been paraded in the plaza of San Miguel, and the ceremony of counting up had been gone through, it was ascertained that the notorious Salezar—the greatest brute among Armijo's officers— was to have charge of us. This was considered unfortunate by all.... The beginning of a cold and disagreeable winter was at hand, as we set off on foot upon a journey of over *two thousand miles*—we were in the hands of a brute whose only delight was in cruelty and blood—should we be fortunate enough to withstand the fatigues attendant upon the journey, an uncertain fate awaited us at its termination; thus, with hope lending hardly a gleam of sunshine to the dark clouds before us, the reader can easily imagine that our condition was gloomy in the extreme.[11]

Governor Lamar's ideas to tap the markets of New Mexico and to reap huge profits from the trade between Cuba and Santa Fe by putting Texans in a kind of "middle-man" position failed miserably. The ill-planned Texan-Santa Fe Expedition, instead of strengthening the claim of Texas that the Rio Grande was its western border, resulted in the deaths and incarceration of many of its participants.[12]

Few issues in American history have generated more political controversy than the annexation of Texas. As early as 1837, President Martin Van Buren had refused a request by

NARRATIVE

OF THE

TEXAN SANTA FÉ EXPEDITION,

COMPRISING A DESCRIPTION OF

A TOUR THROUGH TEXAS,

AND

ACROSS THE GREAT SOUTHWESTERN PRAIRIES, THE CAMANCHE AND
CAYGÜA HUNTING-GROUNDS, WITH AN ACCOUNT OF THE
SUFFERINGS FROM WANT OF FOOD, LOSSES FROM
HOSTILE INDIANS, AND FINAL

CAPTURE OF THE TEXANS,

AND

THEIR MARCH, AS PRISONERS, TO THE CITY OF MEXICO.

WITH ILLUSTRATIONS AND A MAP.

BY GEO. WILKINS KENDALL.

IN TWO VOLUMES.

VOL. I.

NEW-YORK:

HARPER AND BROTHERS, 82 CLIFF-STREET

———

1844.

Title page from Kendall's *Narrative of the Texan Santa Fé Expedition*
(From the author's collection)

the Texas government to be incorporated into the Union as a separate state. Consequently, the matter was dropped. By 1843, however, debate over annexation was becoming more heated. Former President Andrew Jackson, the Tyler administration, John C. Calhoun, and the soon-to-be president James K. Polk, were all in favor of the speedy annexation of Texas. Former President Martin Van Buren and the popular statesman Henry Clay opposed the idea.

Mexico's Santa Anna—by now back in power after his exile following the defeat by Sam Houston at San Jacinto—

General Antonio Lopez de Santa Anna

(From *The Complete History of the Mexican War*, by N.C. Brooks)

threatened war if the United States consummated its plans to annex Texas. Nevertheless, on April 12, 1844, the annexation treaty was signed between officials of the Republic of Texas and John C. Calhoun, President Tyler's secretary of state. However, by the time Congress made the annexation measure official and President Tyler had signed it, Tyler had only three days left on his term as president. James K. Polk was about to enter the White House. Now the fate of Texas was in Polk's hands, and the quiet, diminutive man from Tennessee already knew what he must do when he became president.

James K. Polk was virtually unknown when he was nominated for the presidency. Born in 1795 in North Carolina, he moved to Tennessee as a young man and practiced law in the small town of Columbia, situated about forty miles south of Nashville. Early in his political life, Polk accepted the tenets of "Jacksonian Democracy," and the Tennessean looked toward his friend and neighbor Andrew Jackson as a mentor for his own political philosophies and aspirations. Polk had served in the United States House of Representatives for several years, four of them as speaker. Yet, his was not exactly a household name when he surprised the nation by being nominated at the 1844 Democratic Convention over the party's perennial favorite, former President Martin Van Buren. Defeating the Whig candidate Henry Clay in the fall elections, Polk stepped into the presidency in March 1845.

President Polk left no doubt about his position on westward expansion, in general, and Texas annexation, in particular. He made his stance well known in his inaugural speech of March 4, 1845. From the East Portico of the United States Capitol building, Polk proclaimed:

> The Republic of Texas has made known her desire to come into our Union, to form a part of our Confederacy and enjoy with us the blessings of liberty secured and guaranteed by our Constitution. Texas was once a part of our Country—was unwisely ceded away to a foreign power—is now independent, and

possesses an undoubted right to dispose of a part or the whole of her territory and to merge her sovereignty as a separate and independent state in ours. I congratulate my country that by an act of the late Congress of the United States the assent of this Government has been given to the reunion, and it only remains for the two countries to agree upon the terms to consummate an object so important to both....[13]

Polk attempted to smooth the waters with an angry Mexican government when he added:

Foreign powers should...look on the annexation of Texas to the United States not as the conquest of a nation seeking to extend her dominions by arms and violence, but as the peaceful acquisition of a territory once her own, by adding another member to our confederation, with the consent of that member, thereby diminishing the chances of war and opening to them new and ever-increasing markets for their products.[14]

The new president then let his audience know his exact feelings regarding Texas annexation:

...I shall on the broad principle which formed the basis and produced the adoption of our Constitution, and not in any narrow spirit of sectional policy, endeavor by all constitutional, honorable, and appropriate means to consummate the expressed will of the people and Government of the United States by the reannexation of Texas to our Union at the earliest practicable period.[15]

President Polk's reference to Texas as having once belonged to the United States and his statement referring to the "reannexation" have their origin from his firm belief that Texas was part of the original Louisiana Purchase and that the

President James K. Polk
(From oil painting in the White House)

U.S. relinquished the territory to Spain in 1819 when Spain ceded Florida to the United States.

Polk's political idol Andrew Jackson was ecstatic over the annexation news. A Washington friend wrote to him, "I congratulate you, Dear General, on the success of the great question which you put in action."[16] An elated Jackson, although ill and with only three months to live, replied,

> I not only rejoice, but congratulate my beloved country. Texas is reannexed, and the safety, prosperity, and the greatest interest of the whole Union is secured by this...great and important national act.[17]

Mexican reaction to Polk's address was as expected. On March 6 the Mexican minister to Washington wrote a note to Secretary of State John C. Calhoun, in which he called American plans to annex Texas "an act of aggression, the most unjust which can be found recorded in the annals of modern history."[18] On March 28 the Mexican government suspended diplomatic relations with the United States. During the summer of 1845 General Zachary Taylor—who had already been ordered to the Texas frontier in April 1844, in anticipation of potential trouble with Mexico over the annexation plans— now positioned his 1,500 American soldiers on the south bank of the Nueces River on land claimed by both countries.

On December 29, 1845, less than ten months from the day he took office, President Polk oversaw the official entry of Texas into the Union. In the meantime, Mexican authorities continued to warn officials in Washington that American annexation of Texas would lead to war. On April 24, 1846, Mexican soldiers crossed the Rio Grande and killed eleven American troopers. General Taylor sent a dispatch to Washington in which he proclaimed, "Hostilities may now be considered as commenced."[19]

On May 3 Mexican artillery in Matamoras opened fire on Fort Texas across the Rio Grande, and on May 8 and 9 General Taylor and his American troops encountered Mexican soldiers and won two battles at Palo Alto and Resaca de la Palma. "Mexico has passed the boundary of the United States, has invaded our territory and shed American blood on American soil,"[20] President Polk told a surprised Congress on May 11. Two days later, Congress voted for a declaration of war and earmarked ten million dollars and fifty thousand soldiers for the effort.

The mood of Americans over the declaration of war was mixed. Northern Whigs, especially, adamantly opposed United States involvement in Mexico and saw the entire episode as an exercise in imperialism. Philip Hone, a former mayor of New York City, expressed the attitudes of many of his political allies when he wrote in his diary in early May that:

> Mr. Polk and his party have accomplished their object: the war with Mexico is fairly commenced. The President (in violation of the Constitution, which gives to Congress the exclusive power to declare war) announces formally that a state of war exists, calls for volunteers and money, which Congress unhesitatingly grants; and if any old-fashioned legislator presumes to doubt the authority of Pope Polk, or questions the infallibility of his bull, he is stigmatized by some of the ruffians of the West as an enemy to his country, in league with the Mexicans.[21]

Thomas Hart Benton, the Senate's leading advocate for "westward expansion" and "manifest destiny," disapproved of the manner in which the United States entered the war. President Polk wrote of Benton's feelings in his diary entry for May 11.

> Col. Benton said that the House of Representatives had passed a bill today declaring war in two hours, and that one and a half hours of that time had been occupied in reading the documents which

accompanied my message, and that in his opinion in the nineteenth century war should not be declared without full discussion, and much more consideration than had been given to it in the House of Representatives.[22]

And, John C. Calhoun, who had signed the original annexation treaty with Texas authorities in 1844, opposed the declaration as written and abstained from voting on the war measure in the Senate.

Regardless of public opinion and the criticisms of opposing party members, the war with Mexico had begun. General Taylor was already making the American military presence felt along the Texas-Mexico border, and several states were asked to furnish volunteer militia to augment the United States Army.

Less than a month after the declaration of war was issued, a military command called the "Army of the West" was organized and sent to New Mexico and California to occupy those two Mexican territories. The army's first major goal was the conquest of Santa Fe, a quaint little town claimed by both the state of Texas and the Mexican government.

NOTES—CHAPTER ONE

1. For a well-researched book about Nolan, Wilkinson, and Bean, see John Edward Weems, *Men Without Countries* (New York: Houghton Mifflin Company, 1969).
2. See Walter Prescott Webb and H. Bailey Carroll, ed., *Handbook of Texas* (Austin: Texas State Historical Association, 1952). This work has recently been revised and updated.
3. For more about Austin's colonizing scheme, see *Handbook of Texas*. For an older, but still serviceable, biography of Stephen Austin, see Eugene C. Barker, *The Life of Stephen F. Austin* (Nashville: Cokesbury Press, 1925).
4. The Fredonian revolution is covered at length in William C. Binkley, *The Texas Revolution* (Austin: Texas State Historical Association, 1979).
5. Letter from Andrew Jackson to John Overton, dated June 8, 1829. Quoted in Robert V. Remini, *Andrew Jackson and the Course of American Democracy* (New York: Harper & Row, Publishers, 1981), vol. 2, p. 202.
6. Quoted in Jeff Long, *Duel of Eagles* (New York: William Morrow and Company, Inc., 1990), pp. 16-17, from Gene Brack, *Mexico Views Manifest Destiny* (Albuquerque: University of New Mexico Press, 1975).
7. Quoted in *Duel of Eagles*, p. 18, from José María Sánches, "A Trip to Texas in 1828," published in the *Southwestern Historical Quarterly*, vol. 29, no. 4, (April, 1926).
8. Literature about the fall of the Alamo is plentiful. See especially Jeff Long, *Duel of Eagles*; John Myers Myers, *The Alamo*; Lon Tinkle, *13 Days to Glory*; and Wallace O. Chariton, *100 Days in Texas: The Alamo Letters*.
9. See Binkley, *The Texas Revolution*.
10. The *Austin City Gazette*, issue of April 28, 1841, quoted in Noel M. Loomis, *The Texan-Santa Fé Pioneers* (Norman: University of Oklahoma Press, 1958), p. 3.

11. George Wilkins Kendall, *Narrative of the Texan Santa Fé Expedition* (New York: Harper and Brothers, 1844), Vol. 1, pp. 364-365.

12. George Kendall, *Narrative of the Texan Santa Fé Expedition* and Noel M. Loomis, *The Texan Santa Fé Pioneers*, are the foundation studies on the abortive Texan Santa Fe fiasco.

13. *Inaugural Addresses of the Presidents of the United States* (Washington, D.C.: 101st Congress, 1st Session, Senate Document 101-10, 1989), p. 107.

14. Ibid.

15. Ibid., p. 108.

16. Letter from Frank Blair to Andrew Jackson, dated February 28, 1845, quoted in Remini, *Andrew Jackson and the Course of American Democracy*, 1984, Vol. 3, p. 511. Blair was the editor of the Washington *Globe*, and during Jackson's two terms as president he had served as the administration's official mouthpiece.

17. Letter from Andrew Jackson to Frank Blair, dated March 10, 1845. Ibid.

18. K. Jack Bauer, *The Mexican War, 1846-1848* (New York: Macmillan Publishing Co., Inc., 1974), p. 16.

19. Message from General Zachary Taylor to Adjutant-general Roger Jones, dated April 26, 1846, quoted in K. Jack Bauer, *The Mexican War, 1846-1848*, p. 48.

20. President Polk's message to Congress, quoted in Allan Nevins, ed., *Polk: The Diary of a President 1845-1849* (New York: Longmans, Green and Company, 1952), p. 87, Note 4.

21. Allan Nevins, ed., *The Diary of Philip Hone 1829-1851* (New York: Dodd, Mead and Company, 1927), Volume 2, p. 763.

22. Allan Nevins, ed., *Polk: The Diary of a President 1845-1849*, pp. 87-88.

CHAPTER TWO

THE LAND AND THE PEOPLE

When Texas entered the Union on December 29, 1845, the new entity brought with it the same boundaries as it had maintained as a republic. The state's western border continued to be the Rio Grande River to its source and then a straight line north for three hundred miles. On today's map, this vast region includes parts of the states of Wyoming, Colorado, Kansas, Oklahoma, and New Mexico. During both republic and statehood days, however, the thousands of square miles of territory lying between the Rio Grande and roughly the one hundredth meridian was claimed by Mexico as well.

Immediately after attaining statehood, Texas authorities attempted to organize the disputed lands east of the Rio Grande into counties, to little avail.[1] The far western expanses of the new state were a kind of no-man's-land, claimed by

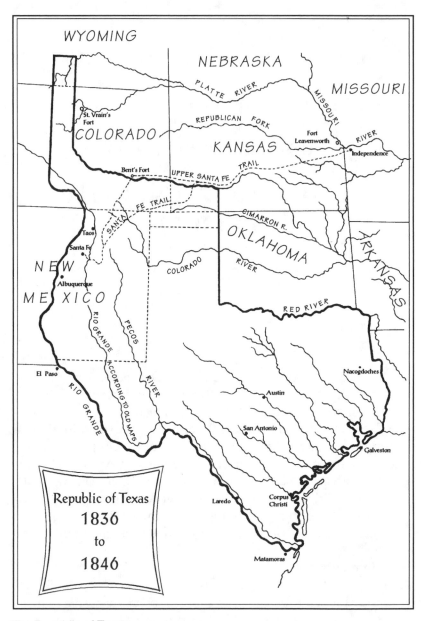

The Republic of Texas

both Texas and Mexico, the former being half-heartedly supported by the United States. Clearly, however, American authorities believed the distant lands belonged to Mexico, since, when war was declared in 1846, explicit orders were issued for an American army to march to Santa Fe (in reality, located in Texas, according to its claims) and to occupy New Mexico for the United States.

Although New Mexico in 1846 plainly lay within the Mexican sphere of influence, Americans had visited the region and traded with its inhabitants for years. Not only was Santa Fe the destination for hundreds of Missouri traders from 1821 on, but Taos became headquarters for several Rocky Mountain fur trappers as well. Some Americans even changed their citizenships and permanently relocated to New Mexico, primarily in Santa Fe and Taos.

Lieutenant Zebulon Pike may have been the first American to set foot on New Mexican soil. In mid-1806 General James Wilkinson, by now governor of Upper Louisiana and the same man who was involved with Philip Nolan in the early Texas filibustering episode, sent Pike on a mission that eventually took the young army officer to Chihuahua. Wilkinson's orders to Pike were for his party to visit several Indian tribes along his route and to uncover as much information as he could about the headwaters of the Red and Arkansas rivers. Wilkinson confided to Pike that this data would be extremely valuable to the United States in determining the boundary line between the recently purchased Louisiana Territory and Spanish holdings in the Southwest. As in the case of the earlier Texas missions, however, it can be assumed that Wilkinson was still gathering information that would assist him with the "Spanish conspiracy." As far as is known, however, Pike was unaware of his commander's interests or intentions.

In February 1807, upon the headwaters of the Rio Grande, Lieutenant Pike was confronted by a troop of Spanish cavalry. "What, is not this the Red River?" asked the surprised Pike in an attempt to convince the soldiers that he was lost. Although treated cordially by the Spanish, Pike and his men were arrested, escorted to Santa Fe, and finally to Chihuahua. During the spring of 1807, he and his command were released from captivity and returned to the United States.

Pike's primary legacy was the propagation of the "Great American Desert" myth that, for years, discouraged many would-be immigrants from casting their fates to the West. In writing of the region through which he passed, Pike suggested that:

> Our citizens being so prone to rambling and extending themselves on the frontiers will, through necessity, be constrained to limit their extent on the west to the borders of the Missouri and Mississippi, while they leave the prairies incapable of cultivation to the wandering and uncivilized aborigines of the country.[2]

Manuel Lisa, a well-known Missouri fur entrepreneur, became interested in the commercial aspects of Santa Fe in 1806, as well. Lisa and his partner, Jacques Clamorgan, a seventy-four-year-old fur trapper and trader from St. Louis, borrowed twelve thousand dollars and outfitted a trading party to travel to "the frontier of New Mexico near the town of Sta. Fe." Along with several companions and four mules loaded with trade goods, Clamorgan and Louison Beaudoin, another St. Louis trader, entered the Spanish town in December 1807, thus establishing themselves as the first American traders to realize a profit from the sleeping Santa Fe trade.[3]

Over the next ten years, several other parties of Missouri traders made trips to Santa Fe. However, because Spanish authorities there were hostile toward Americans and wary of their intense interest in the region, most of the traders were arrested and their goods confiscated.

A bizarre incident occurred during early American attempts to penetrate the Santa Fe trade. It involved three

Missouri traders named Robert McKnight, Samuel Chambers, and James Baird. Their group left St. Louis in the spring of 1812, and when it arrived in Santa Fe later in the year, all of its members were promptly arrested by Spanish officials and their trading goods seized. Most of the men of the expedition were imprisoned until 1821. Adding insult to injury, the Mexicans invoiced the luckless Americans for their daily upkeep while in prison at the cost of 18 3/4 cents per day, to be charged against their own trade goods, now in the hands of the Spanish!

In 1821 an event occurred in Spanish America that dramatically changed the attitudes that government officials and the common people of New Mexico had for Americans. In September, after years of failure, Mexico finally won its independence from Spain and immediately opened the doors of its northernmost province, New Mexico, to any and all Americans who wished to trade. Missouri traders were delighted. Already, one of them, William Becknell, a native Virginian in his early thirties, was on his way to Santa Fe to try his hand at trading in what he thought to be a fabulously rich country.

Becknell had correctly assessed the recently received, sketchy news from Santa Fe that an overthrow of Spain was imminent. Accordingly, in early June 1821, some three months before Mexico officially declared its independence, he advertised in the Missouri *Intelligencer* for men to accompany him on the journey.

> Every man will fit himself for the trip with a horse, a good rifle, and as much ammunition as the company may think necessary for a tour or 3 month trip, & sufficient cloathing [sic] to keep him warm and comfortable.... It is requisite that every 8 men shall have a pack horse, an ax, and a tent to secure them from the inclemency of bad weather....[4]

Becknell's party set out from Arrow Rock, Missouri, on September 1, 1821, only a few days before, unbeknown to anyone in the United States, Mexico would declare its independence. This date marks the real beginnings of American trade with New Mexican citizens and, because of his premier role in the historic event, William Becknell is called the "father" of the Santa Fe trade.

Becknell's outward journey carried him along what is now recognized as the primary route of the Santa Fe Trail. From the Missouri settlements, he entered today's Kansas. Moving southwestward, he passed the future town sites of Council Grove, Fort Larned, and Dodge City. Following the Arkansas River, he and his men moved into Colorado and pressed on southwestward to Raton Pass, located on today's Colorado-New Mexico border. Southward into New Mexico, Becknell's party continued, until it reached the small village of San Miguel and, finally, Santa Fe.

Caravan on the Santa Fe Trail
(From *Commerce of the Prairies*, by Josiah Gregg)

As they neared their destination in November 1821, Becknell and his trading party were approached by soldiers. Apprehensive about the confrontation, the Missourians watched carefully as the troops rode nearer. Thankfully, however, the soldiers warmly greeted Becknell and his men and welcomed them to the newly independent republic of Mexico. Becknell later recorded that:

Although the difference of our language would not admit of conversation, yet the circumstances attending their reception of us, fully convinced us of their hospitable disposition and friendly feelings. Being likewise in a strange country, and subject to their disposition, our wishes lent their aid to increase our confidence in their manifestations of kindness.[5]

Becknell learned from the soldiers that the Mexican people had, in fact, recently won their independence from Spain. Furthermore, he was told that, now, government officials would not only tolerate free trade with the Americans, but that they would actually seek it. Becknell's later meeting with the governor of New Mexico confirmed this information. In his journal, Becknell reported that Governor Don Facundo Melgares "expressed a desire that Americans would keep up an intercourse with that country, and said that if any of them wished to emigrate, it would give him pleasure to afford them every facility."[6]

American traders found a merchant's paradise in New Mexico. Residents of Santa Fe and the other numerous villages that dotted the countryside were isolated by great distances from the large towns and markets in Mexico. Consequently, they relied on their own skills and industry to make a meager living off the dry and sparse land. Trade caravans from Mexico City and other cities to the south were few and far between, and when the first of the American traders arrived on the scene with all kinds of hard-to-find goods, the common folk embraced them enthusiastically.

When Becknell's Missouri traders depleted their limited goods, they left New Mexico for the trip home. After displaying their "rawhide packages of silver dollars" to friends in Franklin, Missouri, Becknell and his men began devising the next year's trip. Since it was already apparent that no one owned a monopoly on the Santa Fe trade at this early date, careful planning was essential. For example, two other American parties had entered Santa Fe just a few days after Becknell reached the town on his first trip. One group was led by trappers named Hugh Glenn and Jacob Fowler, and the other included John McKnight, the brother of Robert McKnight, who, years earlier, had tried his hand at trading with the Mexicans, only to be imprisoned for his efforts. William Becknell wanted his second journey to be better organized and not to be bothered by the competition.

On May 22, 1822, Becknell, along with twenty-one men and three wagons full of top quality trade goods, crossed the Arrow Rock ferry in Missouri, bound for his second trading mission to Santa Fe. The new expedition was a much more grandiose affair than Becknell's original trading party. This time, wagons, instead of mules, were used to carry the freight, and this decision brought with it logistical problems not encountered on the first trip.

After several weeks of hard travel, the Becknell trading party arrived in the neighborhood of today's town of Dodge City, Kansas. Becknell knew that his wagons could not negotiate the steep cliffs and rocky outcroppings that were common throughout Raton Pass. Accordingly, he turned his wagons toward the southwest and drove them across the dry region that lay between the Arkansas and Cimarron rivers and beyond.

The new route, which in later years would be called the Cimarron Cutoff, traversed some extremely desolate country. Josiah Gregg, who will be introduced presently, described this part of Becknell's journey several years later:

The adventurous band pursued their forward course without being able to procure any water, except from the scanty supply they carried in their canteens…. The forlorn band were at last reduced to the cruel necessity of killing their dogs, and cutting off the ears of their mules, in the vain hope of assuaging their burning thirst with hot blood.[7]

Suffering from several grueling days of blistering heat and unquenchable thirst, Becknell's second expedition finally crossed the desert. A few more days' travel found them in the New Mexican village of San Miguel, not far from Santa Fe. Despite the hardships endured by Becknell and his men and animals, his second trading mission proved to be even more successful than the first.

By 1823 several other Missouri traders had convinced themselves that fortunes existed in New Mexico, just for the taking. Consequently, traffic between Missouri and New Mexico continued to grow. During the decade between 1826 and 1835, more than 1,500 men, accompanied by 775 wagons and carrying nearly one and a half million dollars' worth of merchandise, made the arduous journey from the United States to the rich markets at the end of the Santa Fe Trail.

It remained for another man, Josiah Gregg, to document the opportunities offered by the New Mexican markets. Gregg, a Tennessean who was sent west by his physician due to ill health, traveled a total of eight times across the southern plains between Missouri and the New Mexican settlements. Gregg's book *Commerce of the Prairies: Or The Journal of a Santa Fe Trader, During Eight Expeditions across the Great Western Prairies, and a Residence of nearly Nine Years in Northern Mexico* is a storehouse of information about the land, its people and their customs, and wildlife along the Santa Fe Trail and in New Mexico. The book, published in two volumes in 1844, was in large part responsible for the growing awareness of the Santa Fe trade and the presence of the rich markets that existed in New Mexico. In the preface to the two-volume set, Gregg begged his reader's indulgence, admitting that his book "is very far from being what it should be, and what, in more capable hands, it might have been." But, without his informative tome, knowledge about the Trail and its conditions and data regarding the Santa Fe markets would have been sorely lacking among those Americans desiring to make

Josiah Gregg
(From an old daguerreotype)

the long and difficult trip to New Mexico. Gregg died during the Mexican War, never realizing that he had produced one of the all-time classics of American historical travel literature.

It was a great day for Mexicans and Americans alike when a trade caravan pulled into Santa Fe. Josiah Gregg left a moving account of the arrival of one of them. He wrote that the appearance of the wagon train:

> ...produced a great deal of bustle and excitement among the natives. *"Los Americanos!"*—*"Los carros!"*—*"La entrada de la caravana!"* were to be heard in every direction; and crowds of women and boys flocked around to see the new-comers; while crowds of *léperos* hung about as usual to see what they could pilfer. The wagoners were by no means free from excitement on this occasion. Informed of the 'ordeal' they had to pass, they had spent the previous morning in 'rubbing up;' and now they were prepared with clean faces, sleek combed hair, and their choicest Sunday suit, to meet the 'fair eyes' of glistening black that were sure to stare at them as they passed. There was yet another preparation to be made in order to 'show off' to advantage. Each wagoner must tie a bran new 'cracker' to the lash of his whip; for, on driving through the streets and the *plaza pública*, every one strives to outvie his comrades in the dexterity with which he flourishes this favorite badge of authority.[8]

American fur trappers also found the region around Taos and Santa Fe to be lucrative markets for trading their furs and peltries. By the 1830s and 1840s, scores of fur trappers had already discovered Taos and were dealing with its inhabitants in a rapidly developing, profitable business. The Bent brothers, Charles and William, traders from Missouri, realized the reward to be found in the southwestern fur trade. Charles, the future governor of New Mexico, became so enamored with the region, that he relinquished control of Bent's Fort to his brother, moved to Taos, married, and made the town his permanent home. Bent's Fort—built in 1833 by Charles and William, along with another Taos resident, Ceran St. Vrain—sat on the Santa Fe Trail along the north side of the Arkansas River. Soon after the fort's construction, it became the nerve center of a large and prosperous fur enterprise carved out of the wilderness by the Bents and St. Vrain.[9]

Although New Mexico was well populated with Americans by the 1840s, the region was still predominantly a Mexican province, inhabited primarily by Indians and Mexicans with varying degrees of loyalty to the Mexican government. Americans were tolerated because they brought goods from the East that were not readily available in the remoteness of the New Mexican frontier. However, the Mexican government always had, and still did, claim the entire New Mexican region as its own.

Even earlier than Mexicans and Americans, there were yet other peoples who had a tremendous and enduring impact on the culture and history of New Mexico. These were the various tribes of Pueblo Indians, who lived up and down the Rio Grande, and the Spanish conquistadores and their followers, who were the first Europeans to discover and settle the vast Southwest.

Normally peaceful, the Pueblos, for most of their existence, had led defensive lives, protecting themselves from the more warlike southern Plains tribes—the Comanche, Kiowas, and Apache. After the latter people acquired horses from the Spanish in the sixteenth century, they frequently preyed upon the peaceful Pueblos, who were content to live in one spot and raise their corn, beans, squash, and other agricultural produce. The Pueblos lived in multilevel apartment houses, many of which are still in existence today. Descended from the Anasazi, or "ancient ones," their population just

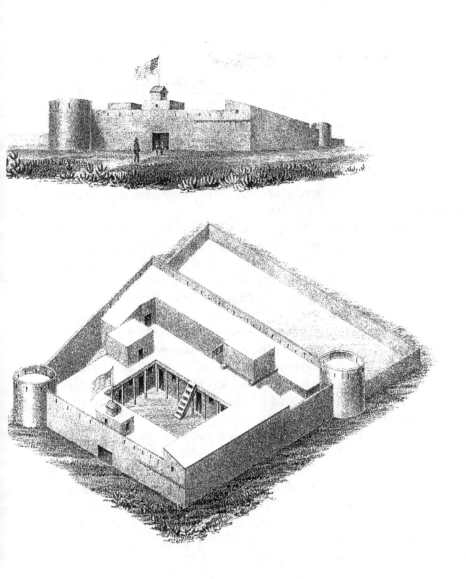

Bent's Fort on the Santa Fe Trail
(From *Journal of Lieutenant J.W. Abert, From Bent's Fort to St. Louis, in 1845*)

before the arrival of the Spanish may have reached forty thousand people.

It was these Pueblo tribes that occupied much of northern New Mexico when the region was first visited by conquistadores under the command of Captain-general Francisco Vasquez Coronado. Coronado and a force of several hundred soldiers and friendly Indians reached the Pueblo village of Hawikul, located in the fabled province of Cíbola, in early July 1540. Another Spaniard, Fray Marcos, had visited Cíbola the previous year and had brought back reports to Spanish authorities that he had seen a town "larger than the city of Mexico." According to Marcos, Cíbola possessed "a great store of gold...and a hill of silver."

Searching for the fabulous riches that Fray Marcos had reported, a disappointed Coronado found only a dusty pueblo, manned by several hundred hostile warriors anxiously perched atop the roofs of the adobe houses. Instead of a town whose inhabitants "wear silk clothing down to their feet," and that contained "a temple of their idols the walls of which... were covered with precious stones," Coronado and his tired command found only scantily clad natives working about their sun-baked apartment houses. Coronado was, indeed, disappointed at his first view of Hawikul, today's Zuni Pueblo, still occupied and located about forty miles south of Gallup, New Mexico.

Coronado sent a soldier, a priest, and an interpreter ahead of his column to read the *requerimiento*, a directive that demanded all the Indians in the entire region to submit to the authority of the Spanish crown and the Catholic Church. For his efforts, the soldier was rewarded with derisive yells and gestures, while the priest was almost hit by an arrow. Finally deciding that a peaceful entry into the pueblo was not forthcoming, Coronado gave his men the order to attack.

A vicious battle ensued, and Coronado quickly realized that his army was up against a formidable enemy. Several soldiers and tribesmen were killed and wounded in the violent battle. After two sorties, the pueblo was finally taken, but not before Coronado, himself, became a casualty. The captain-general later wrote of the bloody conflict.

> They [the natives of Hawikuh] all directed their attack against me because my armor was gilded and glittered and on this account I was hurt more than the rest, and not because I had done more or was farther in advance than the others; for all these gentlemen and soldiers bore themselves well, as was expected of them.[10]

One of Coronado's men, Pedro de Castañeda, confirmed in his journal that the attack on Hawikul was difficult and described his captain's mishap in battle.

> During the attack they knocked the general down with a large stone, and would have killed him but for Don Garcia López de Cárdenas and Hernando de Alvarado, who threw themselves above him and drew him away, receiving the blows of the stones, which were not few....[11]

After the battle, the Spanish soldiers fell upon the pueblo's food stores like hungry animals. Rummaging through the defeated village, the men soon "found that of which there was greater need than of gold or silver, which was much corn, and beans, and fowl better than those of New Spain, and salt, the best and whitest I have ever seen in all my life," according to one eyewitness.

After gorging themselves on the spoils of war, Coronado and his lieutenants discussed their bearings and laid plans for the future. One party, consisting of a dozen horsemen, was sent westward in search of a great river that was rumored to exist far away among the Hopi tribe. Members of that group became the first Europeans to view the Grand Canyon. In the meantime, Coronado decided to send a second party eastward in search of other cities that might prove to be more rewarding than Hawikul. Led by Hernando de Alvarado, this command left the others late in the summer. When he arrived in the vicinity of today's city of Bernalillo, Alvarado sent a message back to Coronado recommending that winter camp be pitched nearby. Then, pushing on eastward, Alvarado soon entered the village of "Cicuye," later known as Pecos Pueblo, and described the town as:

> ...a pueblo containing 500 warriors. It is feared throughout the land. It is a square, perched on a rock in the center of a vast patio or plaza.... The houses are all alike, four stories high. One can walk on the roofs over the whole pueblo, there being no streets to prevent this.... The houses have no doors on the ground floor. The inhabitants use movable ladders to climb the corridors which are on the inner side of the pueblos. They enter them that way, as the doors of the houses open into the corridors on this terrace.... The pueblo is surrounded by a low stone wall. Inside there is a water spring, which can be diverted from them.[12]

Some years later, another Spaniard, Gaspar Castaño de Sosa, described the clothing of the Pecos inhabitants:

> The dress of the men, according to what we saw there—as it was the cold season—most or all of them wore a blanket of cotton and a buffalo hide over it.... The women [dress] with a blanket drawn in a knot at the shoulder and a sash the width of a palm at the waist. At one side, the blanket is completely open. Over it are placed some other very gaily worked blanket or some turkey feather robes and many other curious things....[13]

The majesty of Pecos was not all that interested Alvarado. He was equally intrigued by a story told to him by the natives.

They told him that far off to the east, beyond the great prairies where the buffalo roamed, lay a magical kingdom known as "Quivira," full of the riches that the conquistadores had traveled so far to obtain. When Alvarado reported this wonderful story to Coronado, the Spanish army made immediate plans to seek the fabulous land. Shortly after visiting Pecos himself, during the spring of 1541, Coronado led his tired and weary troops out of New Mexico and into the vast loneliness of the Great Plains. The Indians' ploy worked well. The natives of the Pueblo villages that dotted the landscape of northern New Mexico sighed in relief, as they watched the mighty Spanish army ride toward the eastern horizon searching for a nonexistent paradise.[14]

Soon after Coronado and his soldiers had introduced the ways of Europeans to the frightened natives, he was quickly followed by missionaries anxious to save the souls of all those lost Pueblo peoples. The army and the Church worked hand in hand, and before many years had passed, the landscape of today's Southwest was dotted with missions, churches, and presidios. By 1625 padres had completed a church compound at Pecos. About 300,000 adobe bricks, each weighing forty pounds, were used in the construction. Some of the walls were twenty-two feet thick, and the church itself had six separate bell towers. Indeed, the ways of the Pueblo and the other indigenous peoples were changing dramatically as influences from their Spanish masters spread from tribe to tribe.[15]

By 1680 the Pueblo people had grown tired of the Spanish yoke and attempted to drive the hated Europeans back to Mexico. They succeeded when a member of the Taos Pueblo named Popé organized the warriors of most of the northern villages into a powerful force. The Pueblo Revolt, as the rebellion was called, pitted Indian against Spaniard, and when the insurrection was over, soldier and priest alike had been expelled from New Mexico. Retreating to the area around today's El Paso, the disfranchised Spanish could do little

Seventeeth-century Spanish church at Pecos

(From *Pecos: A Trail Guide to the National Monument, N.M.*, published by the Southwest Parks and Monuments Association)

about their situation as they listened to the many rumors that their one-time neighbors to the north had destroyed all vestiges of the Spanish presence in the region.

For twelve years, the Pueblo people lived in the blissful state that existed among them before the arrival of the Spanish. However, their joy was short-lived. Within twelve years, their old foes from the south returned to reassert themselves as the masters of the Southwest, and this time, they were back for good.[16]

It is obvious, after reviewing the rich and varied early history of the New Mexico region, that, by the time the Mexican War had begun, the area had become a melting pot for three vastly different cultures. Several tribes of Indians—both sedentary Pueblos and the wandering, mounted Apaches—had made the arid countryside their home for hundreds of years and had left a rich tapestry of material culture. The entrance of the Spanish in the sixteenth century, and the acculturation of various Mexican Indian tribes with these newly arrived Europeans to the south, had set the stage for the establishment of Mexico, which after its separation from Spain, spread its influence northward. Finally, the American presence, in the guise of trappers, traders, and professional soldiers, added to the already complicated cultural milieu. It is not surprising, then, with this triangle of cultures—all with such distinctive differences in religion, mores, and lifestyles—that political dissatisfaction, followed by revolt, was just a matter of time.

NOTES—CHAPTER TWO

1. Howard R. Lamar, ed., *The Reader's Encyclopedia of the American West* (New York: Harper & Row, Publishers, 1977), p. 1170.
2. Quoted in William H. Goetzmann, *Exploration and Empire* (Austin: Texas State Historical Association, 1993), p. 51. from Zebulon M. Pike, *The Expeditions of Zebulon Montgomery Pike*, Elliott Coués, editor (New York, 1895).
3. For an authoritative study of Lisa see Richard Edward Oglesby, *Manuel Lisa and the Opening of the Missouri Fur Trade* (Norman: University of Oklahoma Press, 1963).
4. *Missouri Intelligencer*, June 25, 1821, quoted in Larry M. Beachum, *William Becknell, Father of the Santa Fe Trade* (El Paso: Texas Western Press, 1982), p. 17.
5. Quoted in Beachum, *William Becknell*, pp. 28-29, from the *Franklin Intelligencer and Boone's Lick Advertiser*, September 1, 1821.
6. Ibid., p. 29.
7. Josiah Gregg, *Commerce of the Prairies* (New York: Henry G. Langley, 1844) pp. 22-23.
8. Ibid., pp. 110-111.
9. For a comprehensive and detailed history of the Bent, St. Vrain Company and Bent's Fort, see David Lavender, *Bent's Fort* (Garden City: Doubleday & Company, 1954).
10. Quoted in A. Grove Day, *Coronado's Quest: The Discovery of the Southwestern States* (Berkeley: University of California Press, 1964), p. 118, from Francisco Vásquez Coronado, *Relatione che mandó Francesco Vasquez di Coronado, etc.*, translated in George Parker Winship, "The Coronado Expedition, 1540-1542," in *Fourteenth Annual Report*, Bureau of American Ethnology (Washington, D.C.: Government Printing Office, 1896).
11. Quoted in *Arizona Highways*, April, 1984 issue, from Pedro de Castañeda, *Relación de la jornada de Cibola, etc.*, translated in George Parker Winship, "The Coronado Expedition, 1540-1542."

12. John V. Bezy and Joseph P. Sanchez, ed., *Pecos: Gateway to Pueblos & Plains—The Anthology* (Tucson: Southwest Parks and Monuments Association, 1988), pp. 48-49, from Hernando de Alvarado, *Relación de lo que Hernando de Alvarado y Fray Joan de Padilla, etc.*, translated in George Parker Winship, "The Coronado Expedition, 1540-1542."
13. David Grant Noble, "Pecos Pueblo-December 31, 1590" in *Exploration* (Santa Fe: School of American Research, 1981), p. 27, from the translation of Gaspar Castaño de Sosa's journals by Albert H. Schroeder and Dan S. Matson (Santa Fe: School of American Research, 1965).
14. Coronado's travels throughout the American Southwest are detailed in A. Grove Day, *Coronado's Quest: The Discovery of the Southwestern States* and in George Parker Winship, "The Coronado Expedition, 1540-1542." See Note 10.
15. For an in-depth history of Pecos Pueblo, see John L. Kessell, *Kiva, Cross, and Crown: The Pecos Indians and New Mexico, 1540-1840* (Washington, D.C.: National Park Service. U.S. Department of the Interior, 1979).
16. *Kiva, Cross, and Crown* covers the Pueblo Revolt very nicely.

CHAPTER THREE

THE MISSION

At the outset of hostilities with Mexico, Stephen Watts Kearny, a middle-aged United States Army colonel, was ordered to form a command called the "Army of the West," whose mission was to capture New Mexico and California from the Mexicans. To Kearny, the assignment was a challenge that would prove to be the high point of his career.

Kearny, an experienced veteran, was born in New Jersey in 1794. Barely old enough to see service in the War of 1812, he was, nevertheless, commissioned a captain in 1813, and a few years later transferred to the "frontier." His association with mounted cavalry dated all the way back to the original formation of the U.S. Regiment of Dragoons in 1833. At that time, Kearny was promoted to lieutenant colonel and second-in-command of this new mounted branch of the U.S. Army. The dragoons were to be a crack outfit, and admittance to the new unit was limited to "healthy, respectable men, native citizens, not under twenty, nor over thirty-five years of age, size, figure and early pursuits may best qualify them for mounted soldiers."[1]

In 1836, when his commander, Colonel Henry Dodge, resigned from the Army to become governor of Wisconsin Territory, Kearny, himself, assumed command of the Dragoons with the rank of colonel. From that point on and for several years—although during 1836 a second regiment of dragoons was formed—Kearny served as the senior leader of the Army's mounted troops. Kearny's reputation was also enhanced by the Army's reliance on a book he had written.

General Stephen Watts Kearny, 1st Regiment, U.S. Dragoons
(From *The History of the Military Occupation of the Territory of New Mexico from 1846 to 1851 by the Government of the United States,* by Ralph Emerson Twitchell)

Entitled *Carbine Manual of Rules for the Exercise and Maneuvering of U.S. Dragoons*, the volume became the recognized authority on the use and care of American military shoulder arms.

When Stephen Kearny inherited the 1st Dragoons from Colonel Dodge, he immediately assigned the horses in his regiment to the various companies according to their colors. Thus, one could distinguish among companies by the color of the mounts.[2] A stern disciplinarian, Colonel Kearny soon had his regiment whipped into clockwork precision. His adroitness with man and horse did not go unnoticed by his superiors. General Edmund Pendleton Gaines, the commander of the western department of the Army at the time, commented on one occasion that:

> The First Regiment of Light Dragoons at Fort Leavenworth, recently inspected by the Commanding General, was found to be in a high state of police and discipline reflecting the highest credit on Colonel Kearny—the exemplary commandant,—his captains and other officers, non-commissioned officers and soldiers, whose high health and vigilance, with the excellent condition of the horses, affords evidence of their talents, industry and steady habits.[3]

When war was declared with Mexico on May 13, 1846, Colonel Kearny and his 1st United States Dragoons were stationed at Fort Leavenworth, Missouri. On that same day, from Washington, D.C., the secretary of war, William L. Marcy, sent Kearny a copy of the declaration. In a separate letter, the adjutant general of the United States Army, Roger Jones, advised Kearny that a mounted force, most likely to be commanded by Kearny himself, would soon be assembled and sent to Santa Fe in order to protect U.S. citizens and property. A letter, also written on May 13 and signed by the secretary of war, was dispatched to the governor of Missouri, John C. Edwards, requesting him to immediately raise a regiment consisting of eight companies of mounted volunteers and two companies of volunteer artillery. The following day, Adjutant General Jones wrote to Colonel Kearny once again, this time confirming that he was to be the commander of the military force.[4]

Sixteen days later in Washington, President Polk and his cabinet were seriously discussing the advisability of sending an army to New Mexico this late in the season. Although it was only May, Polk was concerned whether the army had time to march to New Mexico, conquer the territory, and then march all the way to California before snow blocked the mountain passes. "In winter, all whom I had consulted agreed that it was impracticable to make the expedition,"[5] wrote President Polk in his diary. Thomas Hart Benton, the senior senator from Missouri, had different ideas. Benton, who only the previous month was hesitant about the speedy manner in which the United States declared war on Mexico, was now one of the leading advocates for the rapid prosecution of the conflict. President Polk continued in his diary:

> Col. Benton had brought me Frémont's [John Charles Frémont, who was Benton's son-in-law] map and book and given me much detailed information of the route and of the difficulties attending it, but advised the expedition this season provided it could move from Independence by the first of August.[6]

Satisfied that Benton knew what he was talking about, Polk continued with his plans.

> I finally submitted a distinct proposition to the Cabinet. Col. Kearny of the United States army was as I learned an experienced officer, and had been with a part of his regiment to the South Pass of the Rocky mountain, and made an extensive tour in that region last year.... The proposition which I submitted was that Col. Kearny should be ordered as soon as he took

Santa Fé, if he thought it safe to do so and practicable for him to reach California before winter, to leave Santa Fé in charge of his Lieutenant-Colonel with a sufficient force to hold it, and proceed towards California with the balance of his command....[7]

Without debate, President Polk's proposition was approved by his cabinet officers. Orders were written to Colonel Kearny, and he received them a few days after the President and his cabinet conferred in Washington. In a letter dated June 3, 1846, from the United States secretary of war, W. L. Marcy, Kearny was advised that:

It has been decided by the President to be of the greatest importance in the pending war with Mexico to take the earliest possession of Upper California. An expedition with that view is hereby ordered, and you are designated to command it.[8]

In the same letter, Kearny was informed that one thousand mounted Missouri troops would follow his command, and that if more soldiers were needed, he had the authority to directly contact the governor of Missouri for assistance.[9]

Kearny was also apprised of the fact that a large group of Mormon immigrants was somewhere on the plains en route to California. "It has been suggested here that many of these Mormons would willingly enter into the service of the United States, and aid us in our expedition against California," wrote Secretary Marcy.[10] Kearny's orders, therefore, included authority to recruit a military force from the Mormons, not to exceed one-third of his entire army. The result was the famous Mormon Battalion that later blazed the trail for Kearny's march from New Mexico to California.

While Marcy's directives left no doubt that President Polk fully expected Kearny to conquer New Mexico and California one way or the other, a peaceful occupation was preferred.

Should you conquer and take possession of New Mexico and Upper California...you will establish temporary civil governments therein.... In performing this duty it would be wise and prudent to continue in their employment all such of the existing officers as are known to be friendly to the United States, and will take the oath of allegiance to them.... You may assure the people of those provinces that it is the wish and design of the United States to provide for them a free government, with the least possible delay, similar to that which exists in our Territories.... In your whole conduct you will act in such a manner as best to conciliate the inhabitants and render them friendly to the United States.[11]

Upon receipt of his orders, one of Colonel Kearny's first tasks was to solicit the assistance of the Mormons. On June 19, 1846, he directed Captain James Allen, one of his officers, to:

...proceed to their camps and endeavor to raise from among them four or five companies of volunteers to join me in my expedition to that country, each company to consist of any number between seventy three and one hundred and nine; the officers of each company will be a captain, first-lieutenant and second lieutenant, who will be elected by the privates and subject to your approval. The companies, upon being thus organized, will be mustered by you into the service of the United States, and from that day will commence to receive the pay, rations and other allowances given to the other infantry volunteers, each according to his rank.[12]

Over the next several weeks, Captain Allen visited the nearby Mormon camps with a petition requesting volunteers to join his commander's unit and assist him in the occupation of California. Many of the Mormon leaders were hesitant at the offer and were concerned about the welfare of the women and children if the men went off to war. However, when the matter was laid before the Mormons' highest official, President Brigham Young, he replied that:

> ...we want to conform to the *requisition* made upon us, and we will do nothing else until we have accomplished this thing. If we want the privilege of going where we can worship God according to the dictates of our consciences, we must raise the Battalion.[13]

By mid-July, Captain Allen, with the obvious assistance of the Mormon leadership, had raised four full companies—about four hundred men—and part of a fifth.

In the meantime, Governor John Edwards of Missouri was busy raising the regiment of volunteers requested by President Polk. Companies of mounted volunteers were formed and filled across the state, and by June 5 they began arriving at Fort Leavenworth where they were soon mustered into the regular service. While at the fort, the new recruits underwent rigorous training in dragoon tactics. John T. Hughes, a member of the 1st Regiment Missouri Mounted Volunteers as the new unit was called, wrote about the training in his book *Doniphan's Expedition; Containing an Account of the Conquest of Mexico*. Hughes explained that:

> For the space of twenty days, during which time portions of the volunteers remained at the fort, rigid drill twice per day, once before and after noon, was required to be performed by them,—in order to render their services the more efficient. These martial exercises, upon a small prairie adjacent to the fort, appropriately styled by the volunteers, "Campus Martis," consisting of the march by sections of four, the sabre exercises, the charge, the rally, and other cavalry tactics, doubtless proved subsequently to be of the most essential service.[14]

**Colonel Alexander W. Doniphan,
1st Regiment, Missouri Mounted Volunteers**

(From *Doniphan's Expedition*, by John T. Hughes)

By June 18 all of the volunteer companies had arrived at Fort Leavenworth. As was the custom in volunteer forces, the men of the regiment elected their commander. The honor fell to Alexander W. Doniphan, who was a well-known lawyer, but who had volunteered in the 1st Missouri as a private. Now, with the rank of colonel, Doniphan was second in command, next to Colonel Kearny, of the entire Army of the West. By the latter part of June, Colonel Doniphan's regiment was ready to march with Kearny's 1st U.S. Dragoons to New Mexico.

With orders in hand Colonel Stephen Watts Kearny rode out of Fort Leavenworth in late June, 1846, accompanied by a mixed army of 1,658 men. Consisting of three hundred troopers of his own 1st Dragoons; 856 mounted riflemen of the 1st Regiment Missouri Mounted Volunteers, under the command of Colonel Doniphan; 250 artillerymen from St. Louis; 145 infantrymen from Missouri; and 107 Laclede rangers from St. Louis, the Army of the West pointed itself toward Bent's Fort, some 537 miles to the west.[15]

The logistics of the first leg of Kearny's mission—to reach Bent's Fort—were mind-boggling. With him were 3,658 mules, 14,904 cattle, 459 extra horses, and 1,556 wagons. His artillery command consisted of twelve 6-pounder cannon and four 12-pounder howitzers.[16] The sheer magnitude of managing men and materiel of such proportions across hundreds of miles of hot, dry prairie was staggering. But the old veteran Kearny, with the same resourcefulness and determination that he had used years earlier to make the 1st Dragoons such a success, prevailed, and the trip to Bent's Fort was uneventful.

For most of the men, the first part of the journey across the plains was rather enjoyable. John T. Hughes described some of the more pleasant moments in his book. He wrote:

> We crossed the river [the Kansas] without loss or accident, and encamped for the night on the west

bank among friendly Shawnees. Some of the Shawnees have large farms, and as fine fields of corn as are to be met with in the States. They also have plenty of poultry, domestic animals, fine gardens, and many of the luxuries of civilized life. Here we obtained milk and butter; also peas, beans, potatoes, and other vegetables. The country between fort Leavenworth and the Kansas, is very fine; the soil is exceedingly fertile,—vegetation is exuberant; and in many places the timber is tall and stately.[17]

As the miles separating the army from Fort Leavenworth lengthened, however, conditions became more severe. On the morning of July 12 the temperature was ninety-five degrees, and mirages fooled the mounted soldiers into seeing water that was not really there. Provisions were running low. Finally, however, the Arkansas River was sighted, and "Horse and man ran involuntarily into the river, and simultaneously slaked their burning thirst."[18] Herds of buffalo appeared on the endless prairies, and many were killed, cooked, and heartily devoured by the hungry soldiers.

In late July, lead elements of the Army of the West approached Bent's Fort. A difficult first part of the army's journey was now over. As the soldiers drew nearer to the fort, mountain man Thomas "Broken Hand" Fitzpatrick, who had guided Colonel Kearny to the Rocky Mountains and back the previous year, rode up with a message for the colonel. Fitzpatrick's message related that New Mexico's governor, Manuel Armijo, the same man who imprisoned the members of the Texan-Santa Fé Expedition in 1841, was presently preparing all parts of New Mexico for the imminent invasion by the American army, and that Colonel Kearny's "movements would be vigorously opposed."[19]

Although the two men had never met, Kearny no doubt remembered Armijo's role in the Texan-Santa Fé Expedition and how he forcibly marched, under armed guard, scores of

The Army of the West

(From *The History of the Military Occupation of the Territory of New Mexico from 1846 to 1851 by the Government of the United States,* by Ralph Emerson Twitchell)

Texans to Mexico City for detention. And, he still had memories of the 1843 attack by a Texas soldier of fortune, Jacob Snively, upon an advance party of Armijo's army that was traveling up the Santa Fe Trail in today's Kansas on its way to protect a Mexican trading caravan. Snively's men killed seventeen Mexicans and captured eighty-two others. Men of Kearny's own 1st United States Dragoons were sent out, under the command of Captain Philip St. George Cooke, to intercept and arrest Snively's men after the incident caused a national uproar.

Governor Manuel Armijo

(From *The History of the Military Occupation of the Territory of New Mexico from 1846 to 1851 by the Government of the United States*, by Ralph Emerson Twitchell)

Armijo was somewhat of a legend in his native New Mexico. His date of birth is unknown. Although he was born into a poor farming family, he quickly rose above his obscure beginnings by adopting a corrupt, albeit rewarding, life that included theft, duplicity, and murder. Armijo had already served as New Mexico's governor on two other occasions, from 1827 to 1829 and from 1837 to 1844. Then, in 1845, he again assumed the office, in addition to the role of commanding general of New Mexico.

Kearny took Armijo's threats into consideration as he now prepared to plot his next move, the actual occupation of New Mexico, in as painless and bloodless a manner as possible.

Bent's Fort had been built in 1833 by Charles and William Bent and Ceran St. Vrain. Charles, the oldest of the four famous Bent brothers, was born in Charleston, Virginia (now West Virginia) in 1799. When he was six years old, he moved to St. Louis with his mother and father, and there, in the town that served as the gateway to the West, he grew to manhood amid the sights and sounds of the trapper and trader communities. When still a young man, Bent joined the Missouri Fur Company and spent considerable time on the upper Missouri River, although his exact position with the company is unknown. Poor success of the Missouri Company caused young Bent to look in other directions for his future, and his sights soon became set on the newly opened Santa Fe trade. Convinced that the wave of the future pointed to the southwest, Bent immediately immersed himself in the New Mexican trade.

Charles Bent's younger brother William was born in St. Louis in 1809. By 1824 William, deeply influenced by Charles, was trapping along the upper reaches of the Arkansas River and was well familiar with the section of the southern Great Plains through which the Santa Fe Trail ran. Ceran St. Vrain, of French descent, was born in Missouri in 1802, and as early as 1825, he was a frequent visitor to Taos in New Mexico.

In 1830 Charles Bent and Ceran St. Vrain organized the Bent, St. Vrain Company, soon to become the foundation for a commercial empire that covered thousands of square miles. When the company built an adobe fort for trading purposes, it was first known as Fort William, after William who supervised its construction. The name was later changed to Bent's Fort. The structure was located in today's state of Colorado, near the town of La Junta.

William Bent was the more wilderness-oriented of the Bent brothers, and he often chose to remain behind at the fort while Charles made the supply trips back and forth to Missouri. In time, William became the major driving force in the day-to-day management of activities at Bent's Fort, and it was he who guided the company through its successful trading operations among the Indian tribes of the southern Great Plains. William married a Cheyenne Indian named Owl Woman and became even more Indian-like in his habits. His influence among the Indians, through his marriage to Owl Woman, did a great deal to enhance the peace between various Plains tribes and the rapidly approaching whites. In the meantime, Charles Bent had established a permanent home in Taos, the small Mexican-Indian village north of Santa Fe. He married an affluent Mexican widow, and even though he retained his American citizenship, he involved himself in the politics of the town and soon became one of its leading citizens.

By the summer of 1846, when the Army of the West approached Bent's Fort, the structure was the hub for the extensive Bent, St. Vrain operations that reached into today's states of Wyoming, Utah, Colorado, New Mexico, Arizona, Texas, Oklahoma, Kansas, and Nebraska. The fort was a citadel in the wilderness and was frequented by mountain men, Missouri and Taos traders, Mexicans, and members of several tribes of Great Plains and Southwest Indians.[20]

Bent's Fort was a magnificent structure built with adobe bricks. The compound measured 142 feet by 122 feet and contained twenty-six rooms that surrounded a small courtyard. Space was provided inside the fort for corrals, wagon sheds, and a blacksmith. Although it was built primarily as a trading post, the fort's strategic location hundreds of miles deep into Indian territory made it necessary that it be able to serve as a defensive structure as well.

Massive walls, with two conical bastions perched on opposite corners, protected the living quarters, storehouses, and well inside. A small cannon was placed in a watch tower above the walls, and an American flag flew proudly from a flagstaff over the gate. A visitor of the time estimated that Bent's Fort could accommodate upwards of one hundred men.

Matthew Field, a reporter for the New Orleans *Picayune*, visited Bent's Fort during the summer of 1839. The newspaperman left a poetic vision of how the adobe stronghold looked. Field wrote,

> Bricks moulded from the prairie clay
> And roasted in the noontide ray.
> Large as the stones of city halls
> From good "Fort William's" strong built walls.
> And trunks and boughs of "Cotton Wood"
> Form gates and beams and rafters good.
> While grass and mud piled closely o'er,
> Forms sheltering roof and sanded floor.
> A strong-barred gate, a rampart wall,
> And Bastions, guard the stock corral,
> And here some fifty inmates dwell
> From year to year content and well.[21]

George Frederick Ruxton, a young Englishman who journeyed throughout much of the American Southwest during the Mexican War, visited the fort in 1847 and left the following description in his book about his western travels.

Bent's Fort is situated on the left or northern bank of the river Arkansa [sic], about one hundred miles from the foot of the Rocky Mountains—on a low and level bluff of the prairie which here slopes gradually to the water's edge. The walls are built entirely of adobes —or sun-burned bricks—in the form of a hollow square, at two corners of which are circular flanking towers of the same material. The entrance is by a large gateway into the square, round which are the rooms occupied by traders and employees of the host. They are small in size, with walls coloured by a white-wash made of clay found in the prairie. Their flat roofs are defended along the exterior by parapets of adobe, to serve as a cover to marksmen firing from the top.... In the centre of the square is the press for packing the furs; and there are three large rooms, one used as a store and magazine, another as a council-room, where the Indians assemble for their "talks," whilst the third is the common dining-hall, where the traders, trappers, and hunters, and all employees, feast upon the best provender the game-covered country affords....

The appearance of the fort is very striking, standing as it does hundreds of miles from any settlement, on the vast and lifeless prairie, surrounded by hordes of hostile Indians, and far out of reach of intercourse with civilized man....[22]

At any particular time, one might find mountain men, members of several of the southern Great Plains Indian tribes, Santa Fe traders, and U.S. Army personnel, all gathered together at Bent's Fort. One of its primary attractions was the savory food served there to weary travelers along the Santa Fe Trail. The kitchen was supervised by Charlotte, a fine black cook from back East, who was known all over the Southwest for her pancakes and pumpkin pie.

Bent's Fort reigned supreme on the Santa Fe Trail for many years. However, as more and more of the wagon traffic began to travel the shorter, smoother Cimarron Cutoff route, and as trapping activity gradually came to a close, the old fort slowly lost its importance as a dominant factor in the Santa Fe trade. The remains of the fort finally became a stop on the Kansas City, Denver, and Santa Fe stage coach line that was operated by Barlow-Sanderson Overland Stage, Mail and Express Company, but not before William Bent and his family packed up their belongings and rode out of the fort, never to return. Some stories even say that Bent, disillusioned by the United States Army's failure to pay him a fair price for the structure, deliberately blew up the fort when he deserted it.

Although Bent's Fort was never designed to accommodate as large a number of men as arrived there in late July, nevertheless, the owners and managers scurried about to insure that the soldiers were as comfortable as possible. For the short time that members of the Army of the West spent at the fort, most of them bivouacked on the flat lands nine miles downstream.

Santa Fe, the target of the first phase of Colonel Kearny's operations, was only about a two weeks' journey from Bent's Fort. So, while the men and animals of his mixed command rested for the upcoming march, Kearny availed himself of the opportunity to compose a directive which he intended to distribute to the native population along the way to Santa Fe. Dated July 31, 1846, the proclamation read:

> The undersigned enters New Mexico with a large military force, for the purpose of seeking union with and ameliorating the conditions of its inhabitants. This he does under instructions from his government, and with the assurance that he will be amply sustained in the accomplishment of this object. It is enjoined on the citizens of New Mexico to remain quietly at their

homes, and to pursue their peaceful avocations. So long as they continue in such pursuits, they will not be interfered with by the American army, but will be respected and protected in their rights, both civil and religious.

All who take up arms or encourage resistance against the government of the United States will be regarded as enemies, and will be treated accordingly.[23]

On August 2, 1846, the Army of the West broke camp at Bent's Fort and began its southwestward march toward Raton Pass. Once on the other side of the Arkansas River, Kearny and his men found themselves on that parcel of land claimed by both Texas and Mexico. For all practical purposes, from this point on, the army was invading enemy territory. Four days later elements of the army approached Raton Pass. First Lieutenant William H. Emory, a topographical engineer with Colonel Kearny's command, wrote in his journal that:

> ...we commenced the ascent of the Raton, and, after marching 17 miles, halted, with the infantry and general staff, within a half mile of the summit of the pass. Strong parties were sent forward to repair the road, which winds through a picturesque valley, with the Raton towering to the left.... The view from our camp is inexpressibly beautiful and reminds persons of the landscape of Palestine.... The road is well-located. The general appearance is something like the pass at the summit of the Boston and Albany railroad, but the scenery bolder, and less adorned with vegetation.[24]

The following day, the crossing was made, and Lieutenant Emory's barometer showed the height of Raton Pass to be 7,500 feet above sea level.

THIRTIETH CONGRESS—FIRST SESSION.

Ex. Doc. No. 41.

NOTES OF A MILITARY RECONNOISSANCE,

F R O M

FORT LEAVENWORTH, IN MISSOURI,

T O

SAN DIEGO, IN CALIFORNIA,

INCLUDING PART OF THE

ARKANSAS, DEL NORTE, AND GILA RIVERS

BY LIEUT. COL. W. H. EMORY.
MADE IN 1846-7, WITH THE ADVANCED GUARD OF THE "ARMY OF THE WEST."

FEBRUARY 9, 1848.—Ordered to be printed.

FEBRUARY 17, 1848.—*Ordered.* That 10,000 extra copies of each of the Reports of Lieutenant Emory, Captain Cooke, and Lieutenant Abert, be printed for the use of the House ; and that of said number, 250 copies be furnished for the use of Lieutenant Emory, Captain Cooke, and Lieutenant Abert, respectively.

WASHINGTON:
WENDELL AND VAN BENTHUYSEN, PRINTERS.
:::::::::::
1848.

Title page of Emory's *Notes of a Military Reconnoissance*
(From author's collection)

Another topographical engineer, Second Lieutenant J.W. Abert, had started out with Colonel Kearny's command, but due to sickness he had to be left behind at Bent's Fort. When he continued his journey to Santa Fe some weeks after Kearny had already departed, Abert, himself, crossed Raton Pass. In his diary he confirmed the difficulty that wagons had in negotiating the treacherous gap in the mountains.

> ...we commenced the passage of one of the most rocky roads I ever saw; no one who has crossed the Raton can ever forget it. A dense growth of pitch pine interferes with the guidance of the teams; in many places the axletrees were frayed against the huge fragments of rock that jutted up between the wheels as we passed; pieces of broken wagons lined the road, and at the foot of the hill we saw many axletrees, wagon tongues, sand-boards, and ox yokes, that had been broken and cast aside.[25]

When Susan Shelby Magoffin, a nineteen-year-old newly-wed and one of a handful of American women who had ever traversed the Santa Fe Trail, crossed the Raton with her trader husband one week after Colonel Kearny's main force had passed, her party was slowed to a speed of one-half mile per hour. "Worse and worse the road!" she lamented. Continuing, Susan explained in her journal that the going got even slower. She wrote:

> They are even taking the mules from the carriages this P.M. and a half dozen men by bodily exertions are pulling them down the hills. And it takes a dozen men to steady a wagon with all its wheels locked—and for one who is some distance off to hear the crash it makes over the stones, is truly alarming. Till I rode ahead and understood the business, I supposed that every wagon had fallen over a precipice. We came to camp about

half an hour after dusk, having accomplished the great travel of *six or eight hundred yards during the day.*[26]

On the day after the Army of the West crossed Raton Pass, Governor Armijo issued a proclamation of his own. Written on August 8, at Santa Fe, the announcement read:

Fellow Countrymen:—At last the moment has arrived when our country requires of her children a decision without limit, a sacrifice without reserve, under circumstances which claim all for our salvation.

Questions with the United States of America which have been treated with dignity and decorum by the supreme magistrate of the Republic, remain undetermined as claimed as unquestionable rights of Mexico over the usurped Territory of Texas, and on account of this it has been impossible to assume diplomatic relations with the government of North America, whose minister extraordinary has not been received; but the forces of that government are advancing in this department; they have crossed the northern frontier and at present are near the Colorado River.

Hear, then, fellow citizens and countrymen, the signal of alarm which must prepare us for battle....

Today...sacred independence, the fruit of so many and costly sacrifices, is threatened, for if we are not capable of maintaining the integrity of our territory, it will all soon be the prey of the avarice and enterprise of our neighbors from the north, and nothing will remain but a sad recollection of our political existence....

Fellow citizens and countrymen, united with the regular army, you will strengthen the sentiments of loyalty among your defenders. Now to the call! Let us be comrades in arms and, with honest union, we shall lead to victory....

Rest assured that your governor is willing and ready to sacrifice his life and all his interests in the defense of his country. This you will see demonstrated by your chief, fellow-countryman and friend.[27]

Once on the other side of Raton Pass, Kearny's men found that travel was much easier, since the land became relatively flat. The Army of the West was now eight days out of Bent's Fort, and Kearny knew that his command was traveling deep into enemy territory. Along the trail, a party of Mexicans, whose mission was to reconnoiter the American forces, was captured. In a humorous aside from the serious business of war, the Mexicans must have made quite a negative impression on Kearny's men. In the words of Emory, "They were mounted on diminutive asses, and presented a ludicrous contrast by side of the big men and horses of the first dragoons." Thomas Fitzpatrick, the famed mountain man who was serving Kearny as a scout "became almost convulsed whenever he turned his well practised [sic] eye in their direction."[28]

In a more sober vein, however, reports of continuing native unrest gradually made their way to the army. Emory wrote on August 10, that:

Mr. Towle, an American citizen, came to headquarters...and reported himself just escaped from Taos. He brought the intelligence that, yesterday, the proclamation of Governor Armijo reached there, calling the citizens to arms, and placing the whole country under martial law; that Armijo has assembled all the Pueblo Indians, numbering about 2,000, and all the citizens capable of bearing arms; that 300 Mexican dragoons arrived at Santa Fe the day Armijo's proclamation was issued, and that 1,200 more were hourly expected; that the Mexicans to a man were anxious for a fight, but that half the Pueblo Indians were indifferent on the subject, but would be made to fight.[29]

On the following day, Lieutenant Emory continued in his journal that:

> Matters are now becoming very interesting. Six or eight Mexicans were captured last night, and on their persons was found the proclamation of the Prefect of Taos, based upon that of Armijo, calling the citizens to arms, to repel the 'Americans, who were coming to invade their soil and destroy their property and liberties;' ordering an enrolment [sic] of all citizens over 15 and under 50.[30]

Two days later, an American named Spry entered Kearny's camp with additional reports of Mexican unrest. Spry had escaped from detention in Santa Fe the night before. He had intelligence that a Mexican army, led by Governor Armijo, was gathering at Apache Canyon a few miles east of Santa Fe, and that the force intended to make a stand against Colonel Kearny's army there.[31] Undaunted, Kearny and his tired men continued their march toward Santa Fe. On August 14, extra precautions were taken among the men, and an order of march was devised so that a battle formation could be formed immediately. Later in the day, a letter from Governor Armijo was delivered to Kearny. Emory's report reveals that the letter, literally translated, stated:

> You have notified me that you intend to take possession of the country I govern. The people of the country have risen en masse in my defence. If you take the country, it will be because you prove the strongest in battle....[32]

On the evening of August 14, the men of the Army of the West made camp on the outskirts of the small village of Vegas, today's town of Las Vegas, New Mexico, located about sixty miles from Santa Fe. Around midnight, information was received by Colonel Kearny that six hundred Mexicans, fully prepared for battle, had assembled at a pass located two miles from the American encampment. At eight o'clock on the morning of August 15, Kearny, who had just received word of his promotion to brigadier general, rode into the village. Amidst the stares of scores of curious farmers and townspeople, General Kearny climbed to the roof of a low building on the plaza and announced the American occupation of New Mexico. In a speech to the awe-stricken Mexicans, Kearny said:

> Mr. Alcalde [the mayor] and the people of New Mexico: I have come amongst you by the orders of my government, to take possession of your country, and extend over it the laws of the United States. We consider it, and have done so for some time, a part of the territory of the United States. We come amongst you as friends—not as enemies; as protectors—not as conquerers [sic]. We come among you for your benefit—not for your injury.
>
> Henceforth, I absolve you from all allegiance to the Mexican government, and from all obedience to General Armijo. He is no longer your governor; I am your governor. I shall not expect you to take up arms and follow me, to fight your own people who may oppose me; but I now tell you, that those who remain peaceably at home, attending to their crops and their herds, shall be protected by me in their property, their persons, and their religion; and not a pepper, nor an onion, shall be disturbed or taken by my troops without pay, or without the consent of the owner. But listen! he who promises to be quiet, and is found in arms against me, I will hang.
>
> From the Mexican government you have never received protection. The Apaches and Navajhoes [sic] come down from the mountains and carry off your sheep, and even your women, whenever they please. My government will correct all this. It will keep off the

General Kearny at Las Vegas, New Mexico

(From *The History of the Military Occupation of the Territory of New Mexico from 1846 to 1851 by the Government of the United States,* by Ralph Emerson Twitchell)

Indians, protect you in your persons and property; and, I repeat again, will protect you in your religion. I know you are all great Catholics; that some of your priests have told you all sorts of stories—that we should ill-treat your women, and brand them on the cheek as you do your mules on the hip. It is all false. My government respects your religion as much as the Protestant religion, and allows each man to worship his Creator as his heart tells him is best. Its laws protect the Catholic as well as the Protestant; the weak as well as the strong; the poor as well as the rich. I am not a Catholic myself—I was not brought up in that faith; but at least one-third of my army are Catholics, and I respect a good Catholic as much as a good Protestant.

There goes my army—you see but a small portion of it; there are many more behind—resistance is useless.

Mr. Alcalde, and you two captains of militia, the laws of my country require that all men who hold office under it shall take the oath of allegiance. I do not wish for the present, until affairs become more settled, to disturb your form of government. If you are prepared to take oaths of allegiance, I shall continue you in office and support your authority.[33]

General Kearny was surprised when none of the Vegas villagers offered resistance. Several of the leading citizens took the oath of allegiance to the United States, and in a matter of hours, the Army of the West departed for its rendezvous with the six hundred Mexican soldiers who supposedly still awaited them in the pass outside the village. However, the information proved to be false, and no Mexican army was to be seen. The men of the 1st Dragoons, anxious for a fight, ended the day somewhat disappointed.

The village of San Miguel was reached the next day, and after General Kearny assembled the officials and leading citizens, he made a speech similar to the one he had given at Vegas. Reports of the massive buildup of the enemy at Apache Canyon became more frequent now, and in the mid-afternoon, a friendly native rode up to General Kearny and exclaimed, "They are in the Cañon, my brave; pluck up your courage and push them out."[34]

On the following day, a rumor reached the American camp that the two thousand Mexican soldiers under Governor Armijo, supposedly gathered at Apache Canyon, had fled. Indeed, they had, and for reasons that only General Kearny and a few of his trusted staff were aware.

"They are in the Cañon, my brave."

(From *The History of the Military Occupation of the Territory of New Mexico from 1846 to 1851 by the Government of the United States,* by Ralph Emerson Twitchell)

On August 1, from Bent's Fort, Kearny had dispatched James Wiley Magoffin, the brother-in-law of Susan Magoffin, accompanied by Captain Philip St. George Cooke, to Santa Fe to meet with Governor Armijo and to attempt to persuade him to allow the Army of the West to enter the city and to occupy New Mexico peacefully. Magoffin had been summoned to Washington, D.C. the previous June and had met with Thomas Hart Benton and President Polk to discuss the possibility of his participation in an effort to keep Kearny's New Mexican campaign as peaceful as possible. President Polk was impressed with Magoffin and wrote in his diary that "he is a very intelligent man and gave me much valuable information."[35] Benton already knew Magoffin as he was one of Missouri's foremost Santa Fe traders. Since Magoffin knew the New Mexican people and the countryside intimately, Benton felt that his presence with the advancing American army "could be of infinite service to the invading force."[36] Magoffin had agreed to assist Kearny and left Washington immediately. It was not until he reached Bent's Fort on July 26, that he met the commander of the Army of the West, as well as his brother, Samuel, and his sister-in-law, Susan. Samuel and Susan had departed Independence, Missouri on June 11, 1846, as part of a large trading caravan on its way to Santa Fe. When the Magoffin wagons reached Bent's Fort, its members had awaited the arrival of Colonel Kearny and his men.

On August 12, the day that Magoffin and Cooke arrived in Santa Fe, Magoffin had met with Governor Armijo and presented him with a letter written by Colonel Kearny from Bent's Fort. The letter told Armijo that the United States was only interested in the part of New Mexico that lay east of the Rio Grande and pleaded with the governor "to submit to fate" and not to resist the American occupation of the city. Although it has never been proven, a monetary bribe may have helped Armijo see the logic of Magoffin's arguments. When the meeting ended, the governor vowed not to resist the American forces. In order to save face with his people, however, he was compelled to act as if he were going to fight the encroachment of Kearny's soldiers. And, from this compulsion came the misleading rumors about the defense of Apache Canyon, the tough letter to Kearny on August 14, promising battle, and the false information about the defense of Vegas. It was all a sham, made up by Armijo, to protect himself from what he knew would be an irate constituency and government if they ever discovered that he had surrendered New Mexico to the Americans without making a pretense to fight.

Missouri trader, James Magoffin

(From *The History of the Military Occupation of the Territory of New Mexico from 1846 to 1851 by the Government of the United States,* by Ralph Emerson Twitchell)

Magoffin later persuaded Governor Armijo's second-in-command, Colonel Diego Archuleta, to offer no resistance to the American takeover, when he pointed out that all of the territory west of the Rio Grande might be his for the taking, since the United States lacked interest in that part of New Mexico. Of course, the falsehood of that statement would soon become apparent to Archuleta when he later read General Kearny's proclamation of August 22, in which it became clear that the United States intended to occupy both banks of the Rio Grande.

In any event, for the time being, the American agent Magoffin had obtained acquiescence to a peaceful takeover of Santa Fe and the rest of New Mexico by American military forces. Therefore, when Apache Canyon was approached by the Army of the West on August 18, General Kearny found that Governor Armijo had, indeed, lived up to his promise and called off the defense of the canyon.[37]

Unaware of the real reason for the retreat of Armijo's army, Lieutenant Emory, the senior topographical engineer with Kearny, later wrote in his report that:

> Reliable information, from several sources, had reached camp yesterday and the day before, that dissensions had arisen in Armijo's camp, which had dispersed his army, and that he had fled to the south, carrying all his artillery and 100 dragoons with him. Not a hostile rifle or arrow was now between the army and Santa Fé, the capital of New Mexico, and the general determined to make the march in one day, and raise the United States flag over the palace before sundown. New horses and mules were ordered for the artillery, and everything was braced up for a forced march. The distance was not great, but the road bad, and the horses on their last legs.[38]

The Army of the West at Apache Canyon

(From The History of the Military Occupation of the Territory of New Mexico from 1846 to 1851 by the Government of the United States,
by Ralph Emerson Twitchell)

Actually, Kearny's command was only twenty-nine miles from Santa Fe, and the arduous drive for the town was begun. When the men had marched about fourteen miles they came upon the defile that Governor Armijo had recently deserted. According to Emory,

It is a gateway which, in the hands of a skilful engineer and one hundred resolute men, would have been perfectly impregnable.

Had the position been defended with any resolution, the general [Kearny] would have been obliged to turn it by a road which branches to the south, six miles from Pecos, by the way of Galisteo.

Armijo's arrangements for defence were very stupid. His abattis was placed behind the gorge some 100 yards, by which he evidently intended that the gorge should be passed before his fire was opened. This done, and his batteries would have been carried without difficulty.[39]

When they reached Armijo's deserted position in the canyon, the soldiers of General Kearny's command were jubilant. Unaware of the secret negotiations in Santa Fe by Magoffin a few evenings before, the proud soldiers gloried in their military prowess, confident that the Mexican army had fled out of fear.

At around noon on August 18, General Kearny was approached by two Mexicans, one of them the acting secretary of state. The men carried a letter from the lieutenant governor—now the acting governor in Armijo's absence—assuring Kearny that he would encounter no resistance, and extending to him any hospitalities that the town could afford. Advance elements of the American army arrived in Santa Fe at around three o'clock in the afternoon, and the rear guard pulled into town three hours later. Lieutenant Governor Juan Bautista Vigil y Alarid and a score of local dignitaries met Kearny and his staff and served them refreshments consisting of wine and brandy.

While the Americans enjoyed the hospitality of the Mexican officials at the ancient Governor's Palace on the Plaza, they watched at sunset as the Mexican flag was lowered and the Stars and Stripes was run up the flagstaff. From the high ground behind the Palace, thirteen cannons saluted the occasion. Afterwards, Kearny's staff was invited to dinner which, according to Emory,

> was served very much after the manner of a French dinner, one dish succeeding another in endless variety. A bottle of good wine from the Passo de Norte, and a loaf of bread was placed at each plate. We had been since five in the morning without eating, and inexhaustible as were the dishes was our appetite.[40]

The Santa Fe that the Army of the West occupied that hot August day in 1846 was a small Mexican town that had been founded in the opening years of the seventeenth century. At the time of its establishment, it was the northernmost town in New Spain. Now, in the mid-1800s, the village numbered between two and three thousand souls, mostly merchants, the clergy, and farmers. Lieutenant Emory recorded in his notes that "...the inhabitants are, it is said, the poorest people of any town in the province." Continuing his description of the village and its people, Emory added:

> The houses are of mud bricks, in the Spanish style, generally of one story, and built on a square. The interior of the square is an open court, and the principal rooms open into it. They are forbidding in appearance from the outside, but nothing can exceed the comfort and convenience of the interior. The thick walls make them cool in summer and warm in winter.

American Army raising the flag over the Palace of the Governors at Santa Fe
(From *The History of the Military Occupation of the Territory of New Mexico from 1846 to 1851 by the Government of the United States,* by Ralph Emerson Twitchell)

The better class of people are provided with excellent beds, but the lower class sleep on untanned skins. The women here, as in many other parts of the world, appear to be much before the men in refinement, and knowledge of the useful arts. The higher class dress like the American women, except, instead of the bonnet, they wear a scarf over the head. This they wear, asleep or awake, in the house or abroad.

The dress of the lower class of women is a simple petticoat, with arms and shoulders bare, except what may chance to be covered by the reboso.

The men who have means to do so, dress after our fashion; but by far the greater number, when they dress at all, wear leather breeches, tight around the hips and open from the knee down; shirt and blanket take the place of coat and vest.[41]

When Lieutenant J.W. Abert arrived in Santa Fe in September, he recorded a vivid description of the Plaza, where most of the town's business and trade were pursued. Abert wrote:

On the north side is the palace, occupying the whole side of the square. On the remaining sides one finds the stores of the merchants and traders, and in the centre of the square a tall flag staff has been erected, from which the banner of freedom now waves. There all the country people congregate to sell their marketing, and one constantly sees objects to amuse. Trains of 'burros' are continually entering the city, laden with kegs of Taos whiskey or immense packs of fodder, melons, wood, or grapes. Our own soldiers, too, are constantly passing and repassing, or mingling with the motley groups of Mexicans and Pueblo Indians.[42]

Another American, John T. Hughes, a volunteer with Doniphan's regiment, reported that, small as Santa Fe was,

Chapter Three

The village of Santa Fe

(From *Report of Lieut. J.W. Abert, of his Examination of New Mexico in the Years 1846-'47*)

the town contained six Catholic churches. But, there were "no public schools, the business of education being entrusted to ecclesiastics." Hughes wrote that "the streets are crooked and narrow," adding that "The whole presents very much the appearance of an extensive brickyard."[43]

The day after the American army arrived in Santa Fe, General Kearny assembled a great many of the town's residents in the Plaza across from the Palace of the Governors and addressed them in much the same fashion as he had the people of San Miguel and Las Vegas. When he completed his talk, the former lieutenant governor, Juan Bautista Vigil y Alarid, took the platform and responded to Kearny's entreaties. Among the points that Vigil made were the fact that:

> The inhabitants of this Department humbly and honorably present their loyalty and allegiance to the government of North America. No one in this world can successfully resist the power of him who is stronger.

Continuing, Vigil added:

> Do not find it strange if there has been no manifestation of joy and enthusiasm in seeing this city occupied by your military forces. To us the power of the Mexican Republic is dead. No matter what her condition, she was our mother. What child will not shed abundant tears at the tomb of his parents?... To-day we belong to a great and powerful nation. Its flag, with its stars and stripes, covers the horizon of New Mexico, and its brilliant light shall grow like good seed well cultivated. We are cognizant of your kindness, of your courtesy and that of your accommodating officers and of the strict discipline of your troops; we know that we belong to the Republic that owes its origin to the immortal Washington, whom all civilized nations admire and respect....In the name,

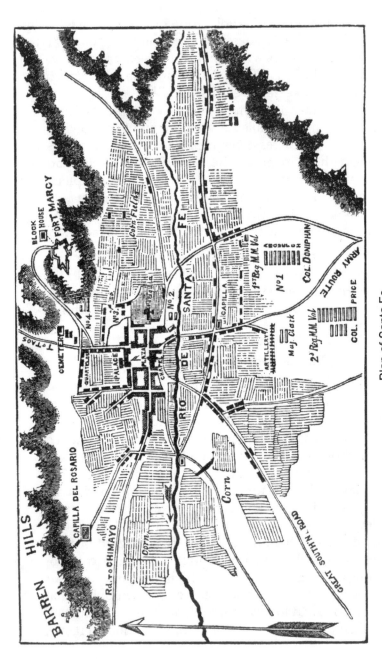

Plan of Santa Fe
(From *Doniphan's Expedition*, by John T. Hughes)

then, of the entire Department, I swear obedience to the Northern Republic and I tender my respect to its laws and authority.[44]

On the next day, August 20, several leaders of the nearby pueblos came to meet with Kearny and to "express their great satisfaction at our arrival."[45] The chiefs gave Kearny their promises of allegiance to the United States, and a gleeful Lieutenant Emory wrote, "They and the numerous half-breeds are our fast friends now and forever."[46] More delegations of local natives visited with Kearny and his staff during the remainder of the week, leaving the Americans with a feeling of security and a job well done.

The American occupation of New Mexico was nearly complete. On August 22 General Kearny issued a proclamation to the people of Santa Fe in which no doubt was left of his expectations.

> As by the act of the republic of Mexico, a state of war exists between that government and the United States; and as the undersigned, at the head of his troops, on the 18th instant, took possession of Santa Fé, the capital of the department of New Mexico, he now announces his intention to hold the department, with its original boundaries, (on both sides of the Del Norte,) as part of the United States, and under the name of 'the Territory of New Mexico.'
> The undersigned has come to New Mexico with a strong military force, and an equally strong one is following close in his rear. He has more troops than necessary to put down any opposition that can possibly be brought against him, and therefore it would be but folly or madness for any dissatisfied or discontented persons to think of resisting him.

The undersigned has instructions from his government to respect the religious institutions of New Mexico—to protect the property of the church—to cause the worship of those belonging to it to be undisturbed, and their religious rights in the implicit manner preserved to them—also to protect the persons and property of all quiet and peaceable inhabitants within its boundaries against their enemies, the Eutaws [sic], the Navajoes [sic], and others; and when he assures all that it will be his pleasure, as well as his duty, to comply with those instructions, he calls upon them to exert themselves in preserving order, in promoting concord, and in maintaining the authority and efficacy of the laws. And he requires of those who have left their homes and taken up arms against the troops of the United States to return forthwith to them, or else they will be considered as enemies and traitors, subjecting their persons to punishment and their property to seizure and confiscation for the benefit of the public treasury.

It is the wish and intention of the United States to provide for New Mexico a free government, with the least possible delay, similar to those in the United States; and the people of New Mexico will then be called on to exercise the rights of freemen in electing their own representatives to the Territorial legislature. But until this can be done, the laws hitherto in existence will be continued until changed or modified by competent authority; and those persons holding office will continue in the same for the present, provided they will consider themselves good citizens and are willing to take the oath of allegiance to the United States.

The United States hereby absolves all persons residing within the boundaries of New Mexico from any further allegiance to the republic of Mexico, and hereby claims them as citizens of the United States. Those who remain quiet and peaceable will be considered good citizens and receive protection—those who are found in arms, or instigating others against the United States, will be considered as traitors, and treated accordingly.

Don Manuel Armijo, the late governor of this department has fled from it: the undersigned has taken possession of it without firing a gun, or spilling a single drop of blood, in which he truly rejoices, and for the present will be considered as governor of the Territory.[47]

General Kearny was obviously pleased with himself and his Army of the West. He had fulfilled the first part of his orders to the letter, and all the better without bloodshed. On the same day that Kearny issued his proclamation, he also sent a letter to General Jonathan E. Wool, the American commander at Chihuahua. In it he proudly reiterated, "I have to inform you, that on the 18th instant, without firing a gun or spilling a drop of blood, I took possession of this city, the capital of the department of New Mexico."[48]

General Kearny expressed the prevalent mood of most American authorities in Santa Fe, when he continued:

Every thing here is quiet and peaceable. The people now understand the advantages they are to derive from a change of government, and are much gratified with it.[49]

In order to bolster the American defense of Santa Fe, General Kearny directed that a fort be built. Placed in command of the site selection were Lieutenant William Emory of the Topographical Engineers and Lieutenant Jeremy F. Gilmer of the Corps of Engineers. An elevated site some six hundred yards northeast of the Plaza, the same position from which the cannons were fired when the American flag was raised over the Palace of the Governors on August 18, was selected and work was begun on August 23. Lieutenant Emory thought that the site was "unfavorable for the trace of a regular work, but being the only point which commands the entire town, and which is itself commanded by no other, we did not hesitate to recommend it."[50]

The construction was supervised by Lieutenant Gilmer and L.A. Maclean, a civilian volunteer in Colonel Doniphan's Missouri regiment. Small details of army enlisted men performed most of the work until August 27, when one hundred more troopers were assigned to the task. Four days later, twenty Mexican stone masons were recruited and added to the crew. Designed to handle a garrison of 280 men, the structure was named Fort Marcy, in honor of United States Secretary of War William L. Marcy.[51]

A few weeks later, when Lieutenant J.W. Abert visited the completed Fort Marcy, he described it as:

> ...situated on a prominent point of the bluffs commanding the city. The distance of the centre of this work, from the flag-staff in the plaza, is but 664 yards. The whole of the interior is defiladed from all the surrounding heights within range; 10 guns may be brought to bear upon the city. The slopes are revetted with adobes. The blockhouse and magazine are constructed of pine logs one foot square. The only approachable point is guarded by the block-house, which also assists to protect the entrance of the fort.[52]

In 1912, years after old Fort Marcy had been deactivated and the property turned over to the Interior Department, L. Bradford Prince described the dimensions of the bastion.

> The extreme length of the fort proper was 270 feet, and its width was 180 feet; the total length between the exterior walls of the surrounding moat was 400

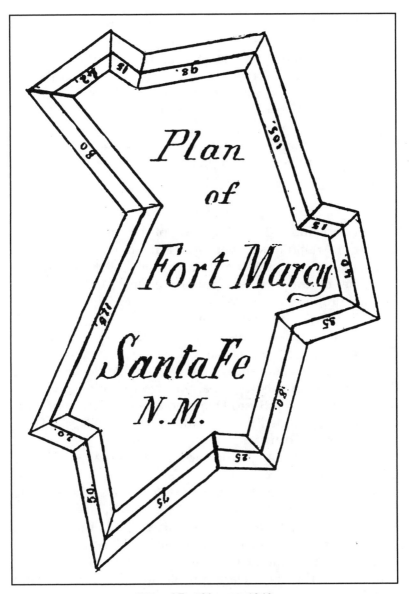

Plan of Fort Marcy—1846

(From *Old Fort Marcy*, by L. Bradford Prince)

feet, and width 300 feet. The gateway was directly to the east, and opposite to that was the redoubt or block house just one hundred feet distant and nearly square in form, with extreme dimensions of 85 feet on the north, south and west, and 95 feet on the east. At the northeasterly corner of this redoubt was a tower, for observation; and this is still the highest and most favorable point from which to enjoy the wonderfully extensive view around the whole circle of the horizon.[53]

On September 2, on the basis of a rumor that former Governor Armijo was gathering an army to march north and attack the Americans, General Kearny, several of his staff, and a number of dragoons left Santa Fe to meet him and to tour the surrounding countryside. They proceeded down the Santa Fe River, crossed over the desert to Galisteo Creek, and from there marched to the stream's confluence with the Rio Grande, near the town of Santo Domingo. Then, the detail traveled the short distance to Santo Domingo Pueblo, where the men were greeted by a party of rowdy, colorfully decorated natives. From Santo Domingo Pueblo, Kearny and his command descended the Rio Grande to the villages of San Felippe and Angosturas.

By September 4, in the vicinity of Bernallilo, Kearny received intelligence that Armijo's rumored buildup was most likely a ruse. Over the next few days, the soldiers marched uneventfully as far south as the village of Tome, located between today's cities of Belen and Albuquerque, before returning to Santa Fe on September 11. Four days later, a small detail departed for Taos, some sixty miles north of Santa Fe and the site of a large pueblo, to reconnoiter the land and determine the condition of the road connecting the two towns.[54]

L E Y E S

DEL

TERRITORIO DE NUEVO MEJICO.

SANTA FE, A 7 DE OCTOBRE 1846.

L A W S

OF THE

TERRITORY OF NEW MEXICO.

SANTA FE, OCTOBER 7 1846.

Title page of General Kearny's *Laws of the Territory of New Mexico*, also known as Kearny's Code

(From the author's collection)

Just before he departed for California, General Kearny performed two important acts. On September 22 he appointed several people to civil offices, as follows:

Charles Bent—governor

Donaciano Vigil, cousin of the former lieutenant-governor under Armijo—secretary of the territory

Richard Dallam—marshal

Francis P. Blair, son of former President Andrew Jackson's journalistic mouthpiece in Washington, Frank Blair—United States district attorney

Charles Blumner—treasurer

Eugene Seitzendorfer—auditor of public records

Joab Houghton, Antonio José Otero, Charles Beaubien—judges of the superior court[55]

On the same day, Kearny sent to Washington officials a copy of the *Laws of the Territory of New Mexico*, which were to be officially published in Santa Fe on October 7. The laws were written by Colonel Alexander W. Doniphan and Private Willard P. Hall, both members of the 1st Missouri Volunteers and both renowned criminal lawyers in their native state. Translation of the code into Spanish was performed by Captain David Waldo, also of the 1st Missouri Volunteers and a prominent Santa Fe trader before the war.[56]

On September 25 General Kearny, with three hundred of his own 1st United States Dragoons, left Santa Fe for the second part of his mission: the conquest of California. He was soon to be followed by the Mormon Battalion, under the command of Captain Cooke. The 1st Missouri Volunteers under Colonel Doniphan were to remain in Santa Fe until relieved by the 2nd Missouri Volunteers, led by Colonel Sterling Price and expected in Santa Fe any day. After Price's arrival, Doniphan was to march to Chihuahua where his regiment would become a part of General Wool's army. Half the artillery was to accompany Doniphan when he departed for Chihuahua and half was to remain in Santa Fe.[57]

NOTES—CHAPTER THREE

1. Gregory J.W. Urwin, *The United States Cavalry: An Illustrated History* (Poole, Dorset, U.K.: Blandford Press, 1983), p. 56.
2. Ibid., p. 73.
3. Ibid.
4. Ralph P. Bieber, ed., *Marching With the Army of the West, 1846-1848* (Philadelphia: Porcupine Press, 1974), pp. 23-24.
5. Allan Nevins, ed., Polk: *The Diary of a President*, 1845-1849, p. 107.
6. Ibid.
7. Ibid.
8. James K. Polk, *Occupation of Mexican Territory. Message from the President of the United States* (Washington D.C., 1846) 29th Congress, 2d Session, Executive Document 19, p. 5.
9. Ibid.
10. Ibid.
11. Ibid., p. 6.
12. Philip St. George Cooke, *The Conquest of New Mexico and California in 1846-1848* (Chicago: The Rio Grande Press, Inc., 1964), p. iv.
13. Ibid., p. viii.
14. John T. Hughes, *Doniphan's Expedition; Containing an Account of the Conquest of New Mexico* (Cincinnati: J.A. & U.P. James, 1850), pp. 25-26.
15. Ibid., p. 27.
16. Urwin, *The United States Cavalry: An Illustrated History*, p. 82.
17. Hughes, *Doniphan's Expedition*, p. 32.
18. Ibid., p. 47.
19. Ibid., p. 56.
20. Refer to David Lavender, *Bent's Fort*, for an excellent treatment of the Bent brothers, Bent's Fort, and the Bent, St. Vrain Company.

21. John E. Sunder, ed., *Matt Field on the Santa Fe Trail* (Norman: University of Oklahoma Press, 1960), pp. 44-45.
22. George Frederick Ruxton, *Life in the Far West*, Leroy R. Hafen, ed. (Norman: University of Oklahoma Press, 1951), pp. 179-181.
23. Polk, *Occupation of Mexican Territory*, p. 19.
24. William H. Emory, *Notes of a Military Reconnoissance, from Fort Leavenworth, in Missouri, to San Diego, in California, Including Part of the Arkansas, Del Norte, and Gila Rivers* (Washington, D.C.: Wendell and Van Benthuysen, Printers, 1848) Executive Document 41, p. 18.
25. James W. Abert, *Report of Lieut. J.W. Abert, of His Examination of New Mexico, in the Years 1846-'47* (Washington, D.C., 1848) 30th Congress, 1st Session, Executive Document 23, p. 25.
26. Susan Shelby Magoffin, *Down the Santa Fe Trail and Into Mexico*, Stella M. Drumm, ed. (Lincoln: University of Nebraska Press, 1962), p. 80.
27. Ralph Emerson Twitchell, *The Military Occupation of New Mexico, 1846-1851* (Denver: The Smith-Brooks Company, Publishers, 1909), pp. 60-63.
28. Emory, *Notes of a Military Reconnoissance*, p. 21.
29. Ibid., pp. 21-22.
30. Ibid., p. 23.
31. Ibid., p. 25.
32. Ibid., pp. 25-26.
33. Ibid., pp. 27-28.
34. Ibid., p. 29.
35. Magoffin, *Down the Santa Fe Trail and into Mexico*, p. xxiv, from Milo M. Quaife, *The Diary of James K. Polk during His Presidency, 1845 to 1849* (Chicago, 1910), p. 474.
36. Thomas Hart Benton, *Thirty Years' View; or, A History of the Working of the American Government for Thirty Years, From 1820 to 1850* (New York: D. Appleton and Company, 1856), Vol. 2, p. 683.

37. For excellent coverage regarding the events surrounding the secret meetings between the American agent, Magoffin, and Mexican authorities, see the passages about the incident in the following: Bernard De Voto, *The Year of Decision: 1846* (New York: Book-of-the-Month Club, Inc., 1984); Paul Horgan, *Great River: The Rio Grande in North American History* (New York: Rinehart & Company, Inc., 1954); and David Lavender, *Bent's Fort* (Garden City, New York: Doubleday & Company, Inc., 1954).
38. Emory, *Notes of a Military Reconnoissance*, pp. 30-31.
39. Ibid., p. 31.
40. Ibid., p. 32.
41. Ibid., pp. 34-35.
42. Abert, *Report of Lieut. J.W. Abert*, p. 32.
43. Hughes, *Doniphan's Expedition*, p. 91.
44. Twitchell, *The Military Occupation of New Mexico, 1846-1851*, p. 75.
45. Emory, *Notes of a Military Reconnoissance*, p. 33.
46. Ibid.
47. Polk, *Occupation of Mexican Territory*, pp. 20-21.
48. Ibid., p. 21.
49. Ibid., pp. 21-22.
50. Emory, *Notes of a Military Reconnoissance*, p. 32.
51. Ibid.
52. Abert, *Report of Lieut. J.W. Abert*, p. 38.
53. L. Bradford Prince, *Old Fort Marcy* (Santa Fe: New Mexican Printing Company, 1912), p. 9.
54. Emory, *Notes of a Military Reconnoissance*, pp. 36-43.
55. Polk, *Occupation of Mexican Territory*, p. 26.
56. Nolie Mumey, ed., *Laws of the Territory of New Mexico* (Denver: Nolie Mumey, 1970), p. iii.
57. Emory, *Notes of a Military Reconnoissance*, p. 45.

CHAPTER FOUR

THE REVOLT

If Stephen Watts Kearny was guilty of making only one mistake during his brief stay in occupied New Mexico, it was his error in judgment relative to the peaceful attitudes of the natives. The general had reaffirmed his feeling of the pacifist mood of most New Mexicans on September 16, 1846, when he wrote in a letter to the adjutant general that they

> ...were found to be highly satisfied and contented with the change of government, and apparently vied with each other to see who could show to us the greatest hospitality and kindness.
>
> There can no longer be apprehended any organized resistance in the Territory to our troops; and the commander of them, whoever he may be, will hereafter have nothing to attend to but to secure the inhabitants from further depredations from the Navajoe [sic] and Eutaw [sic] Indians....[1]

Content that affairs in New Mexico were under control as a result of the threats, bribes, and by the impressions left by his well-heeled Army of the West, General Kearny proceeded to California. But, Kearny could not have been more wrong in his favorable assessment of the situation in Santa Fe and the rest of occupied New Mexico. Underneath the thin veneer of joy and contentment expressed by many of the natives toward their American conquerors, a powder keg of hatred and boiling rebellion was about to explode.

In late 1846, several weeks after Kearny marched off to California, the army intercepted intelligence detailing an anticipated revolt in the region by native Indians and Mexicans. Throughout the following weeks, bits and pieces of information were gathered by military authorities about this potential threat to security. Finally, an informer came forth and revealed the secret plot to the Americans, who promptly attempted to arrest the ringleaders. Santa Fe was in a frenzy when its residents finally realized that a potential revolt had been aborted. Lieutenant James Abert was out of town when the news of the failed uprising became public. When he arrived back in Santa Fe on the morning of December 23, however, he wrote in his journal that:

> Here we found all our friends in a high state of excitement from the discovery of an intended revolution. The guards were posted in all directions, all the guns placed in the Plaza, and everyone in a state of great vigilance. Five of the rebels had been taken and were in prison; two others, T. Ortiz and Archiletta [sic], were keenly pursued. The revolutionizers had a very well-organized plot. Detachments were to march at dead of night and surround the houses of the Governor, Col. Price, and Maj. Clark, while another party seized the guns. The whole body of the troops were to be massacred.[2]

Diego Archuleta

(From *The History of the Military Occupation of the Territory
of New Mexico from 1846 to 1851 by the Government of the
United States*, by Ralph Emerson Twitchell)

The fact that they had barely averted a catastrophe in
which many American citizens might have been killed was
taken rather casually by the commanders. Although troops
were put on extra alert and guards were posted more con-
spicuously, senior officials treated the whole affair with an
almost cavalier attitude. Lieutenant Abert remarked in his
diary entry of December 24, that despite the seriousness of the
situation in Santa Fe, the artillery was being packed up to
accompany Colonel Doniphan. Abert lamented, "But I think
it doubtful whether the safety of this place does not require
that the artillery should remain here."[3] On the same day,
Abert heard that "San Miguel is in a state of insurrection, and
the whole country seems ripe and ready for any hellish
scheme to tear down the Stars and Stripes...."[4]

One of the organizers of the intended revolt, the man referred to as "Archiletta" in Abert's passage, was the same Diego Archuleta who had earlier been led to believe by James Magoffin that the west bank of the Rio Grande could be his to control in return for his cooperation during the occupation of the eastern part of New Mexico by American forces. Naturally, when Archuleta came to realize that General Kearny intended to occupy both banks of the Rio Grande, he believed he had been betrayed and understandably became a key player in the proposed revolution.

Repeated efforts by the army to capture Archuleta failed, and on Christmas day, Lieutenant Abert wrote that:

> We heard that Lt. Walker was in quite a dangerous situation, as he had no more than 13 men with him when he started to arrest Diego Archilette [sic]. In the afternoon while we were at the quarters of Col. Price we heard of his arrival and he soon entered. He had not been successful in catching his prisoner. When at the home of the pursued, the people about collected in considerable numbers, as many as 90 to 100, and seemed half inclined to attack....[5]

The other primary organizer of the suppressed revolt, Tomas Ortiz, made good his escape also, fleeing first to Galisteo and then to Chihuahua.

It was later determined that some of Santa Fe's leading citizens had taken part in the planning of the failed uprising. The Pino brothers, Miguel and Nicholas, along with Manuel Antonio Chaves and a local churchman, Father Antonio José Martinez, all participated in the clandestine affair. Martinez, according to New Mexico's early historian, Ralph Emerson Twitchell,

> realized that the coming of the American was a death blow to his power and prestige in the country and he is said to have used all his power to incite a

sentiment of suspicion and distrust of the American people....No one, except those who were actually engaged as principals in the insurrection, knew positively just what part Fr. Martinez took in the uprising. He was a very crafty man and the American authorities never could affirmatively fix upon him any active participation, although in later years there were many native citizens, who had been identified with the movement, who did not hesitate to declare that they had been guided by his counsel and advice.[6]

Father Antonio Martinez

(From *The History of the Military Occupation of the Territory of New Mexico from 1846 to 1851 by the Government of the United States*, by Ralph Emerson Twitchell)

After the failure of the uprising, however, all but Father Martinez took the oath of allegiance to the United States and served their new country well for the rest of their lives.

The quelling of the intended revolt set for late December, 1846, and the dispersal of the willful participants in the Ortiz-Archuleta affair no doubt went a long way toward convincing American officials in Santa Fe that most, if not all, danger of a significant uprising was over. On December 26 a lavish party was thrown at the Governor's Palace, and the young, impressionable Lieutenant Abert was there.

> We had a grand feast, and all of the luxuries of an eastern table were spread before us. At the sutler's one can get oysters, fresh shad, preserves, and fine champagne. In fact, we concluded that reveling in the halls of the Armijos was far above reveling in the Halls of Montezuma, for the latter was a poor uncivilized Indian, while [the former] boast of being descended from the nobility of Castile.[7]

But, unbeknown to the partying officers of the Army of the West, serious unrest still prevailed in the capital city and in the surrounding countryside. If the Americans had been fooled into believing that all was well, then all the better for two other malcontents, Tomacito, an Indian, and Pablo Montoya, a Mexican, who were busy fanning the fires of hatred in the hearts of every native who would listen to them. Assisted by Jesus Tafoya, Pablo Chavis, and Manuel Cortez, Tomacito and Montoya secretly went about gathering forces to support a revolution of their own. By mid-January, 1847, they had readied their operation for action.

The newly appointed American governor, Charles Bent, although concerned about the recent state of affairs that had just culminated in the squashing of the Ortiz-Archuleta plot the previous month, left Santa Fe for his home in Taos, sixty miles north, on January 14. With him were the sheriff, Stephen Lee; the circuit attorney, James W. Leal; and a prefect, Cornelio Vigil. The ill-fated trip would prove to be all of these men's last.

Bent had maintained a residence in Taos since the mid-1830s when he removed himself from the day-to-day trading existence at Bent's Fort. He had married a well-to-do Mexican widow, Maria Ignacia Jaramillo, and settled in a small adobe house north of the Plaza.[8] Bent had quickly established himself as a man of importance and influence in Taos. Although he did not relinquish his United States citizenship, as some American traders did, he worked actively in the civic affairs of the little town and even became closely acquainted with the Mexican governor, Manuel Armijo, the man he would one day succeed in the palace at Santa Fe.

After the first revolution attempt in December 1846, Governor Bent had issued a proclamation to the people of New Mexico in which he pleaded with them not to foolishly throw away the benefits of their new citizenship by supporting or participating in any future overthrow effort. He told them that reports of a Mexican army on its way north to liberate New Mexico were untrue, and he urged them "to turn a deaf ear to such false doctrines and to remain quiet, attending to your domestic affairs, so that you may enjoy under the law all the blessings of peace...."[9]

Bent also took the occasion to send details about the failed uprising to Secretary of State James Buchanan. Dated December 26, 1846, Bent's letter stated in part:

> On the 17th instant I received information from a Mexican friendly to our Government that a conspiracy was on foot among the native Mexicans, having for its object the expulsion of the United States troops and the civil authorities from the Territory. I immediately brought into requisition every means in my power to ascertain who were the movers in the rebellion, and have succeeded in securing seven of the secondary

conspirators. The military and civil officers are now in pursuit of the two leaders and prime movers of the rebellion; but as several days have elapsed, I am apprehensive that they will have made their escape from the Territory.[10]

Governor Bent finished his letter to Secretary Buchanan on a sinister note. He wrote:

The occurrence of this conspiracy at this early period of the occupation of the Territory will, I think, conclusively convince our Government of the necessity of maintaining here, for several years to come, an efficient military force.[11]

Although he was aware of and extremely concerned about the underlying unrest in the area, Charles Bent had no idea that his personal safety was in jeopardy. In retrospect, it is perhaps understandable why the governor maintained such a naivete about the danger that threatened his very life. He was guilty of refusing to believe that his friends and associates of the past dozen years would imperil him and his family over a political issue. Bent was something of an amateur doctor, and on many occasions, he had come to the rescue of man, woman, and child in his remote hometown. Surely, the bond of human helping human meant something, even if he and most of his neighbors were not of the same national origin.

The fact that his wife, Maria, was a Mexican and related in one way or another to many of the town's most influential residents was another reason for Bent to disregard any serious danger in which his new role as governor might place him. Finally, his own children carried Mexican blood in their veins and were cousins to several other children in Taos. When he considered all of these facts, Charles Bent had no doubt, that if a final call for allegiance came—to him as friend, neighbor, and benefactor, or, to hard feelings over frivolous differences in political ideologies—he would win out.

These thoughts no doubt ran through Charles Bent's mind as he reached his Taos home, tired from his long, cold journey from Santa Fe. Almost immediately upon his arrival, Bent was confronted by a delegation of Indians from the nearby pueblo who requested that he prematurely release two of their neighbors from jail. Was this a test for Bent to determine if his newly assumed duties as governor would stand in the way of performing a favor for his neighbors? The Indians received their answer quickly as Bent replied that he could not interfere with the processes of the law and that the matter would be handled accordingly.

Charles Bent had always loved his little hometown which was sometimes called Don Fernando de Taos, or simply, Don Fernando.[12] Dick Wootton, a mountain man who frequented the village, recalled years later that its population was about five or six thousand, but this figure, recollected by Wootton more than forty years after he was active in the region, is no doubt incorrect. Other descriptions of the period picture Taos as a small village, punctuated with only a few adobe houses and one church fitted with two towers. It is doubtful that more than seven or eight hundred people inhabited the town in 1847. Of the nearby pueblo, Wootton wrote:

> The Pueblo de Taos was an Indian village about two miles from the town. It consisted of one large Pueblo building, six or seven stories high, and a church, which stood some little distance away, both built of adobe. I suppose there were something like a thousand Indians in the Pueblo.... [13]

Charles Bent had spent precious little time with his wife and children, when during the early morning hours of January 19, he was awakened and confronted in his doorway by a band of loud, angry local Mexicans and Indians from the nearby Taos Pueblo. Even in his hour of peril, Bent refused to

"Uncle Dick" Wootton

(From *"Uncle Dick" Wootton*, by Howard L. Conard)

believe that his friends and acquaintances of so many years would harm him. Making no effort to defend himself, Bent attempted to defuse the mob and to talk its participants out of doing anything foolish. Within moments, he realized his mistake.

While pleading with the crowd, Bent was shot in the chin and in the stomach. After gaining entry into the house, several Indians in the mob shot arrows into Bent's body, and as he writhed in pain on the floor, he managed to free three of them from his face. Several of the angry participants slashed Bent's wrists and hands. In the meantime, Mrs. Bent, along with her sister, Mrs. Kit Carson; Mrs. Thomas Boggs; the Bent children; and an old Indian woman, managed to cut a hole through one of the thick adobe walls, using only a poker and a spoon. In the courtyard, they found temporary respite from the violence. The governor, in his dying moments, followed them to the outside.[14]

The attackers soon surrounded the survivors in the courtyard, where Bent died momentarily after being scalped while still alive. Then, his head was severed from his body as his wife and children watched in horror. The Bent family was spared, and according to the governor's daughter Teresina, the murderers "then left us alone with our great sorrow."[15] Instructions were issued to Bent's Mexican neighbors to offer no assistance to the stricken women and children. Teresina continues:

> We were without food and had no covering but our night-clothing, all that day and the next night. The body of our father remained on the floor in a pool of blood. We were naturally frightened, as we did not know how soon the miscreants might return to do us violence. At about three o'clock the next morning, some of our Mexican friends stole up to the house and gave us food and clothing. That day, also, they took my father to bury him....[16]

The revolutionaries were not content with just the American governor's blood. Before they had finished their dark deeds, they murdered and mutilated five more Americans and Mexicans with American loyalties. Pablo Jaramillo, the brother of Mrs. Bent, and Narciso Beaubien, the circuit judge's son, tried to hide in a nearby stable, but their refuge was given away by a Mexican woman who watched as members of the mob pierced the young boys' bodies with lances. A prefect, Cornelio Vigil; the circuit attorney, J.W. Leal; and the sheriff, Stephen Lee, were also murdered on that horrible January morning.[17]

Their brutal deeds done at Taos, the angry Mexicans and Indians now cast their eyes on other nearby American-occupied regions. At Arroyo Hondo, a few miles north of Taos, a Kentucky-born, Missouri-bred trader named Simeon Turley lived with his wife and children. Turley, a man in his early forties, had moved to New Mexico in 1830, and his compound at Arroyo Hondo consisted of a combination distillery, mill, trading post, and home. Turley's Mill was a frequent resting place for mountain men, Indians, Mexicans, and weary travelers. His whiskey was known far and wide, and customers came from miles around to bargain for the almost pure alcohol. Like his friend Charles Bent, Turley was married to a Mexican woman, and the relationship between him and his Indian and Mexican neighbors had always been one of mutual respect and friendship.

On January 19, 1847, when Turley received news of the massacre at nearby Taos, he was having a reunion—in fact, a sort of indoors, old-time rendezvous—with several of his mountain men friends from the past. A few months later, George Ruxton, an English writer best remembered for his firsthand accounts of the mountain men and their way of life, wrote of Turley's situation:

Turley had been warned of the intended insurrection, but had treated the report with indifference and neglect, until one morning a man…made his appearance at the gate on horseback, and, hastily informing the inmates of the mill that the New Mexicans had risen and massacred Governor Bent and other Americans, galloped off.[18]

Turley and his guests immediately set about taking security precautions. The gates to the compound were closed, windows to the casa and outbuildings were barricaded, and rifles were gathered and made ready. Nine men, including Turley, were present at the mill and waiting later in the day as a large party of Mexicans and Indians rode up to the compound and demanded that Turley surrender his American friends. No harm would come to Turley himself, the revolutionaries promised. Ruxton relates that "To this summons Turley answered that he would never surrender his house nor his men, and that, if they wanted it or them, 'they must take them' "[19]

The impasse then began. Turley's Mill was admirably situated for defense. According to Ruxton:

> The building lay at the foot of a gradual slope in the sierra, which was covered with cedar-bushes. In front ran the stream of the Arroyo Hondo, about twenty yards from one side of the square, and on the other side was broken ground, which rose abruptly and formed the bank of the ravine. In rear, and behind the still-house, was some garden-ground enclosed by a small fence, and into which a small wicket-gate opened from the corral.[20]

Nevertheless, the odds against Turley and his men were overwhelming. Several hundred rebels poised outside the walls of Turley's compound, ready to attack the grizzled old mountain men inside. Turley would not budge. He had meant what he said, and soon after he refused to surrender his friends and it became apparent to the assailants that there would be no peaceful victory, the attack was launched.

The fighting continued all day, and as nighttime approached, the Mexican and Indian attackers pulled back and planned how they might finish off the mill the next morning. All night long, the vigilant inhabitants of the compound kept busy standing watch and "running balls, cutting patches, and completing the defences [sic] of the building...."[21]

Vicious fighting commenced early the next morning, by which time the enemy forces had increased in strength. It was soon discovered that, during the night, several rebels had occupied part of the courtyard. As the fighting continued, two defenders were killed, and as the day progressed for the weary Americans, their ammunition began to run out. Fire was then set to some of the outbuildings, and Turley decided that further defense of the compound was useless in the wake of such overwhelming odds.

The survivors inside Turley's Mill discussed the rapidly worsening situation and decided that every man should attempt to escape the compound on his own. As the fighting continued, one by one attempted freedom, but in the end, only three succeeded, and the rest were killed inside.[22] Turley, John Albert, and Thomas Tobin successfully escaped the mill, but Turley was caught and murdered a few miles away when he revealed himself to an old Mexican friend in whom he erroneously believed he could trust. John Albert marched night and day until he arrived at the site of present-day Pueblo, Colorado and informed a group of mountain men there of the massacre. Thomas Tobin escaped to Santa Fe, whose residents had already heard the grisly details of the killings at Taos and at Turley's Mill.[23]

The old mountain man Dick Wootton was at Pueblo when John Albert arrived with the sad news of the demise of Turley's Mill. Years later Wootton recalled that many of his dearest friends had been among those killed in Taos and at

Turley's. Believing that he "should...do something toward securing punishment of their murderers....five of us...started across the country" to offer whatever assistance they could to American authorities in Taos.[24]

To add to the slaughter on that bloody nineteenth day of January, 1847, several rebels killed two other mountain men at Rio Colorado, a few miles north of Turley's Mill. The men,

Mountain man at Turley's Mill

(From *The History of the Military Occupation of the Territory of New Mexico from 1846 to 1851 by the Government of the United States,* by Ralph Emerson Twitchell)

named Harwood and Markhead, were on their way to Taos on a trading trip when they were captured by the Mexicans and Indians. George Ruxton, the writer, noted that:

> They had hardly...left the village when a Mexican, riding behind Harwood, discharged his gun into his back: Harwood, calling to Markhead that he was 'finished,' fell dead to the ground. Markhead, seeing that his own fate was sealed, made no struggle, and was likewise shot in the back by several balls. They were then stripped and scalped and shockingly mutilated, and their bodies thrown into the bush by the side of the creek to be devoured by the wolves.... [25]

On January 19 rebels also attacked the small village of Mora, situated about thirty-five miles southeast, as the crow flies, from Taos. The reports of American casualties vary. Several Missouri traders had just reached the town, totally unaware that the local natives had risen up against their American conquerors. Romulus Culver, Ludlow Waldo, and Lewis Cabano, along with a Mr. Noyes and a Mr. Prewit of Santa Fe and several other Americans were among those killed. [26] Two days later, a United States Army detail in charge of grazing the dragoons' horses in the vicinity of Mora was also attacked and several soldiers killed. [27]

Colonel Sterling Price, who had marched the 2nd Missouri Mounted Volunteers across the Santa Fe Trail and arrived in the capital city in late September, was now in command of the town and the remaining army of occupation. When news of the various massacres of American citizens reached him the next day, he went into immediate action. Price's activities over the next two weeks, during which time he busied himself with all-out reprisal attacks against the strongholds of the revolting Mexicans and Indians, are detailed in the next chapter. As he planned to depart Santa Fe on this important mission, however, he must have realized the truth in the words that he would later write to the adjutant general in Washington. The colonel pretty well summed up the entire matter when he exclaimed, "It appeared to be the object of the insurrectionists to put to death every American and every Mexican who had accepted office under the American government."[28]

NOTES—CHAPTER FOUR

1. Polk, *Occupation of Mexican Territory*, pp. 24-25.
2. John Galvin, ed., *Western America in 1846-1847: The Original Travel Diary of Lieutenant J.W. Abert* (San Francisco: John Howell-Books, 1966), p. 74.
3. Ibid.
4. Ibid.
5. Ibid.
6. Twitchell, *The Military Occupation of New Mexico, 1846-1851*, p. 134-136.
7. Galvin, ed., *Western America in 1846-1847*, p. 75.
8. Lavender, *Bent's Fort*, p. 165.
9. Twitchell, *The Military Occupation of New Mexico, 1846-1851*, p. 125.
10. *Insurrection Against the Military Government in New Mexico and California, 1847 and 1848* (Washington, D.C.: Government Printing Office, 1900), 56th Congress, 1st Session, Senate Document No. 442, p. 6.
11. Ibid.
12. T.M. Pearce, ed., *New Mexico Place Names: A Geographical Dictionary* (Albuquerque: The University of New Mexico Press, 1975), pp. 162-163.
13. Howard Louis Conard, *"Uncle Dick" Wootton* (Chicago: W.E. Dibble & Co., 1890), p. 175.
14. Twitchell, *Military Occupation of New Mexico, 1846-1851*, pp. 126-127.
15. McNierney, ed., *Taos 1847*, pp. 14-15, quoted from Ralph Emerson Twitchell, *The Leading Facts of New Mexican History* (Cedar Rapids: Torch Press, 1912).
16. Ibid., p. 15, quoted from Twitchell, *The Leading Facts of New Mexican History*.
17. Hughes, *Doniphan's Expedition*, p. 393. It is interesting that Charles Bent, Narciso Beaubien, Cornelio Vigil, and Stephen Lee—all of whom were killed in the Taos outbreak—as well as Bent's business partner, Ceran St. Vrain, were holders of large land grants in present-day

northern New Mexico and southern Colorado. Ironically, these grants were awarded to them by Governor Armijo. See David J. Weber, *The Mexican Frontier 1821-1846* (Albuquerque: University of New Mexico Press, 1982), pp. 190-195 for an accounting of these land grants.

18. McNierney, ed., *Taos 1847*, p. 17, quoted from G.F. Ruxton, *Adventures in Mexico and the Rocky Mountains* (London: J. Murray, 1847).
19. Ibid., p. 18, quoted from Ruxton.
20. Ibid.
21. Ibid., p. 19.
22. *Doniphan's Expedition*, by John T. Hughes, p. 393, lists the men killed at Turley's Mill as: "S. Turley, A. Cooper, W. Harfield, L. Folque, P. Roberts, J. Marshall, and W. Austin." Colonel Sterling Price's report to the Adjutant General on February 15, 1847, lists the dead as: "Simeon Turley, Albert Turbush, William Hatfield, Louis Tolque, Peter Robert, Joseph Marshall, and William Austin."
23. Conard, *"Uncle Dick" Wootton*, p. 180.
24. Ibid., p. 179.
25. McNierney, ed., *Taos 1847*, p. 16, quoted from Ruxton, *Adventures in Mexico and the Rocky Mountains*.
26. Letter of Captain W.S. Murphy to Colonel Sterling Price, dated January 25, 1846, in *Insurrection*, p. 20. Letter of Captain I.R. Hendley to Colonel Sterling Price dated January 23, 1847, in *Insurrection*, pp. 18-19. Government Proclamation published in Santa Fe, dated February 15, 1846, in *Insurrection*, pp. 24-26.
27. Ibid., pp. 18-19. Letter of January 23, 1846, from Captain I.R. Hendley to Colonel Sterling Price.
28. Colonel Sterling Price's report to the Adjutant General, dated February 15, 1847, in *Insurrection*, pp. 8-13.

CHAPTER FIVE

RETALIATION

The unleashed fury of the revolutionaries at Taos, Rio Colorado, and Mora on January 19, 1847, and at Turley's Mill on that day and the next, constituted the major effort on their part to, once and for all, destroy anyone and anything related to the American presence in northern New Mexico.

Word about the killings at Taos reached Colonel Sterling Price at Santa Fe the next day, and the Missouri volunteer immediately set about to place the army on full alert and to prepare his troops for a rapid and thorough retaliation at Taos. Concerned that utilizing all of the Santa Fe garrison would leave the town unprotected in the event of continued outbreaks of violence, Price called up other Missouri Volunteer and regular army elements from Albuquerque. Major D.B. Edmonson, of the 2d Missouri, and Captain I.H.K. Burgwin,[1] of the 1st Dragoons, quickly led their men north to Santa Fe, with orders for Burgwin to join Price on his march to Taos and for Edmonson to stay in Santa Fe. When Price determined that the garrison at Santa Fe was well secured, he made his final preparations to leave the capital city.[2]

Donaciano Vigil, the acting governor of New Mexico following the murder of Governor Bent, issued a proclamation from Santa Fe on January 22, urging all citizens of the territory to cease their resistance to the Americans.

Today or tomorrow a respectable body of troops will commence their march for the purpose of quelling the disorders of Pablo Montoya, in Taos. The Government is determined to pursue energetic measures toward all the refractory until they are reduced to

Donaciano Vigil, successor to Governor Charles Bent

(From *The History of the Military Occupation of the Territory of New Mexico from 1846 to 1851 by the Government of the United States*, by Ralph Emerson Twitchell)

order, as well as to take care of and protect honest and discreet men; and I pray you that, hearkening to the voice of reason, for the sake of the common happiness and your own preservation, you will keep yourselves quiet and engaged in your private affairs.[3]

Colonel Price left Santa Fe on his mission of reprisal on January 23. He was accompanied by Companies D, K, L, M, and N, all elements of the 2d Missouri Volunteers. Also present was the Missouri battalion of infantry under the command of Captain Angney and a company of Santa Fe volunteers, commanded by Captain Ceran St. Vrain, the business partner of

Colonel Sterling Price,
2d Regiment, Missouri Mounted Volunteers

(From *Doniphan's Expedition*, by John T. Hughes)

Charles Bent. Lieutenant A.B. Dyer was placed in command of four mountain howitzers. All told, Colonel Price's effective fighting force numbered three hundred fifty-three, all of them dismounted except St. Vrain's volunteers.[4]

Price and his little army had traveled only about twenty-five miles north, toward Taos, when on the following day, January 24, at about 1:30 in the afternoon, Captain St. Vrain's advance scouts discovered that the enemy had fortified the village of Cañada (today's Santa Cruz).[5] Colonel Price immediately made plans to attack. The rebels had occupied the highlands overlooking the road that led from the south into town, and Price ordered his artillery to shell their positions. The American supply trains lagged behind the troop movement, and when this was discovered by the revolutionaries, they attempted to cut the wagons off from the rest of the troops, but they failed in this endeavor. In his report to the adjutant general, dated February 15, 1847, Price described the heated action.

> A charge was then ordered to be made upon all the points occupied by the enemy in any force. Captain Angney with his command, supported by Lieutenant White's company, charged up one hill, while Captain St. Vrain's company turned the same in order to cut off the enemy when in retreat. The artillery, supported by Captains McMillen, Barber, and Slack, with their respective companies, at the same time took possession of some houses (enclosed by a strong corral densely wooded with fruit trees, from which a brisk fire was kept up by the enemy) and of the heights beyond them. Captain Halley's company was ordered to support Captain Angney. In a few minutes my troops had dislodged the enemy at all points, and they were flying in every direction. The nature of the ground rendered pursuit hopeless, and it being near night I ordered the troops to take up quarters in the town. The number of the enemy were about 1,500.

A Missouri Mounted Volunteer

(From *Doniphan's Expedition*, by John T. Hughes)

Lieutenant Irvine was wounded. In the charge my loss was 2 killed and 6 wounded—of the killed one was a teamster who volunteered in Captain Angney's company.[6]

The enemy lost thirty-six men in the battle, one of whom was Jesus Tafoya, one of the ringleaders of the revolt in Taos.

On the following morning, the rebels initially appeared that they would give additional resistance, but after Colonel Price personally led a column in pursuit, they retreated from their positions and left the region.

Two days later, after resting and regrouping at Cañada, Colonel Price and his men resumed marching toward Taos. Now, Price's command was reinforced by Captain Burgwin's company of 1st U.S. Dragoons from Albuquerque and another company of Missouri Mounted Volunteers. With four hundred seventy-nine men, Price continued north along the east bank of the Rio Grande. As the army approached the small village of Embudo, situated along a narrow road that snaked through a deep canyon, Price's men were confronted by around sixty to eighty guerrillas, nestled in the rocks that lined the steep canyon walls. Captain Burgwin was dispatched with one hundred eighty men to flush them out. As Burgwin proceeded down the canyon, he discovered that enemy forces numbering about six or seven hundred had taken up positions along the steep cliffs of a mesa situated between the road to Embudo and the river. The countryside was so rough that the movement of wagons and artillery was practically impossible. Colonel Price described what happened next in his report to the adjutant general.

> The rapid slopes of the mountains rendered the enemy's position very strong, and its strength was increased by the dense masses of cedar and large fragments of rock which every where offered them shelter. The action was commenced by Captain St. Vrain, who, dismounting his men, ascended the mountain on the

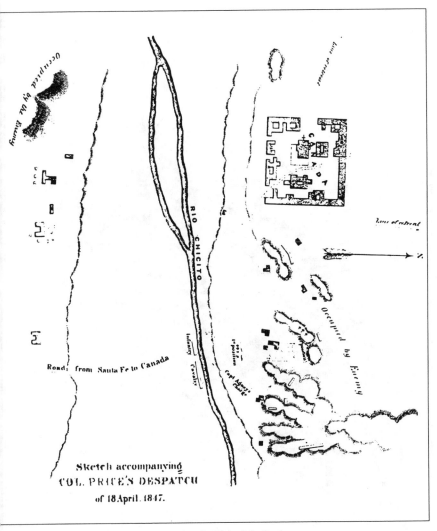

Plan of the Battle of Cañada

(From *Insurrection Against the Military Government in New Mexico and California, 1847 and 1848*)

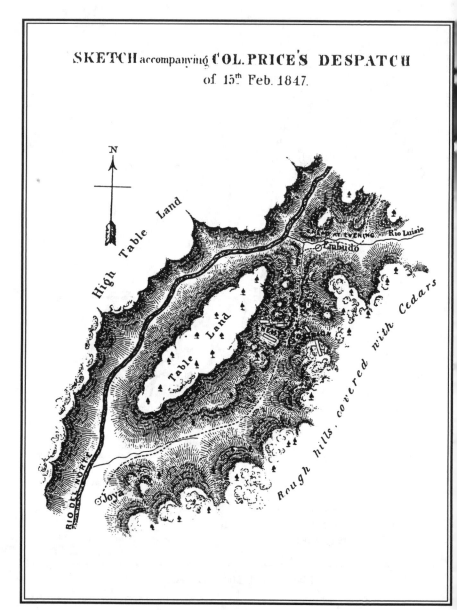

Plan of the Battle of Embudo

(From *Insurrection Against the Military Government in New Mexico and California, 1847 and 1848*)

left, doing much execution. Flanking parties were thrown out on either side, commanded respectively by Lieutenant White, 2d regiment Missouri mounted volunteers, and Lieutenants McIlvaine and Taylor, 1st dragoons. These parties ascended the hills rapidly, and the enemy soon began to retire in the direction of Embudo, bounding along with a speed that defied pursuit.[7]

When Captain Burgwin reached the far side of the defile, he and his men entered the valley in which Embudo was situated. Burgwin recalled his men "and entered that town without opposition, several persons meeting him with a white flag."[8] Despite the heated fighting, only one American was killed and one wounded, compared to twenty enemy killed and sixty wounded.[9]

While Colonel Price and his command were fighting their way up the Rio Grande valley between January 23 and January 29, more conflict was in progress at Mora, thirty-five miles southeast of Taos across the Sangre de Christo Mountains.

Anticipating trouble in the region, Captain I.R. Hendley, in charge of a grazing detachment at Las Vegas, wrote to Colonel Price on January 23. In his letter, the captain reported that:

> To-morrow I expect to go against Mora with part of my force, where it is reported that the Mexicans are embodied. Our ammunition is very short, there only being about 10 rounds of cartridges and 25 pounds each powder and lead....It is of great importance that I should be quickly supplied.
>
> If you will forward me one or two pieces of artillery, well manned, and plenty of ammunition, I pledge myself to subdue, and keep in check every town this side of the mountains.[10]

On January 25, before receiving a response to his request for aid from Colonel Price, Captain Hendley and eighty American troops marched on Mora to restore order after rebels had murdered the Missouri traders there on January 19. Hendley was met by a large contingent of Mexicans prepared to defend the village. During the next hour or so, Hendley's men and the Mexicans fought door to door and at close quarters. When the rebels holed up in an old fort, the Americans were unable to dislodge them without artillery. In the effort, however, Captain Hendley was killed and a couple of soldiers were wounded. The Mexicans suffered twenty-five killed and seventeen taken prisoner. In retaliation for Hendley's death, his successor, Captain Morin, along with his command and one cannon, returned to Mora on February 1 and completely leveled the town.[11]

At about the same time that Mora was being razed by Captain Morin, Sterling Price was finally approaching his destination, the recently terrorized village of Taos. Price later recalled that:

> On the 1st of February, we reached the summit of the Taos mountain, which was covered with snow to the depth of two feet; and on the 2d, quartered at a small village called Rio Chicito, in the entrance to the valley of Taos. The marches of the 1st and 2d were through deep snow. Many of the men were frostbitten, and all were very much jaded with the exertions necessary to travel over unbeaten roads, being marched in front of the artillery and wagons in order to break a road through the snow.[12]

After eleven days of travel over the cold, snowy, rugged countryside of northern New Mexico and following two pitched battles in which several of his men were killed and wounded, Colonel Price and his army finally arrived in Taos

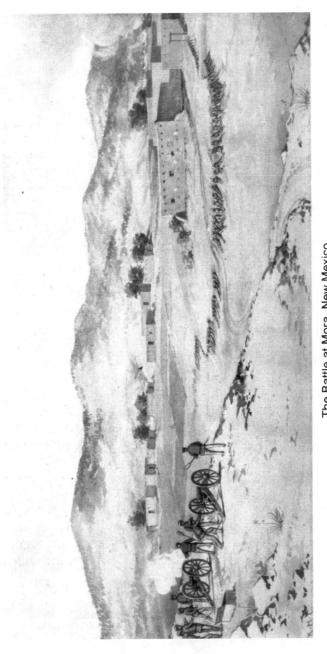

The Battle at Mora, New Mexico

(From *The History of the Military Occupation of the Territory of New Mexico from 1846 to 1851 by the Government of the United States* by Ralph Emerson Twitchell) on February 3. The well-trained Missourian wasted no time in getting down to the business that brought him here.

> ...finding that the enemy had fortified themselves in the Pueblo de Taos, [I] proceeded to that place. I found it a place of great strength, being surrounded by adobe walls and strong pickets. Within the enclosure and near the northern and southern walls, arose two large buildings of irregular pyramidal form to the height of seven or eight stories. Each of these buildings was capable of sheltering five or six hundred men. Besides these, there were many smaller buildings, and the large church of the town was situated in the northwestern angle, a small passage being left between it and the outer wall. The exterior wall and all the enclosed buildings were pierced for rifles. The town was admirably calculated for defence [sic], every point of the exterior walls and pickets being flanked by some projecting building....[13]

Price immediately realized upon viewing the pueblo that its capture was going to be difficult. Even with artillery, he knew that breaching the thick walls of the buildings would be no easy matter. A captain in the Missouri Light Artillery, Woldemar Fischer, explained the invulnerability of the adobe walls to cannon fire in a letter to the adjutant general. Fischer wrote:

> The structure of the houses...is such as to make the use of mortars necessary that will throw a shell of at least 50 pounds. The walls are generally 3 feet thick and built of 'adobes,' a sort of sun-dried brick of a very soft quality through which a ball of a 12-pounder will pass without doing any more damage....[14]

At two o'clock in the afternoon of February 3, Price ordered an artillery attack on the western flank of the church.

The field howitzers and the 6-pounder cannon fired round after round at the strong building from a distance of 250 yards. Nightfall approached rapidly, and the men—cold, tired, and nearly out of ammunition—retired from the battle until the next morning, with little sense of accomplishment. Colonel Price spent the night in Taos.

Price and his men were up early the next morning to again storm the pueblo. The howitzers were divided between Captain Burgwin's command, which was ordered to a position about 260 yards west of the church, and Lieutenant Dyer, who took a position with most of the remainder of the army some 300 yards from the northern wall of the pueblo. Captains St. Vrain and Slack, along with their mounted volunteers and dragoons, proceeded to the eastern end of the pueblo, with orders to cut down any rebels who tried to get away in that direction.

For two hours, the artillery banged away at the church, with very little effect. At around 11:00 A.M., Captain Burgwin and two companies of dragoons charged the western wall of the sanctuary, while Captain Angney's infantry and a contingent of Missouri Volunteers attempted to breach the northern wall. While the American soldiers hacked away at the church's formidable adobe walls, someone brought up a ladder and set fire to the building's roof. In the confusion, Captain Burgwin was killed.

Finally, under cover of the 6-pounder cannon firing grape shot into the town, soldiers cut several small holes into the church's walls and manually threw artillery shells into the building. Then, at about 3:30 P.M., the 6-pounder was brought to within sixty yards of the church, and its crew zeroed in on one of the holes in the wall. After ten rounds, the artillery fire enlarged the hole appreciably. The grand finale of the battle for the church was reported by Colonel Price.

> The gun was now run up within ten yards of the wall—a shell was thrown in—three rounds of grape were poured into the breach. The storming party...

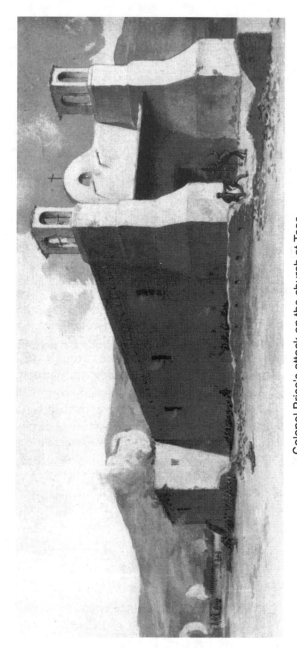

Colonel Price's attack on the church at Taos

(From *The History of the Military Occupation of the Territory of New Mexico from 1846 to 1851 by the Government of the United States* by Ralph Emerson Twitchell) entered and took possession of the church without opposition.... A few of the enemy were seen in the gallery where an open door admitted the air, but they retired without firing a gun. The troops left to support the battery on the north were now ordered to charge on that side. The enemy abandoned the western part of the town. Many took refuge in the large houses on the east, while others endeavored to escape toward the mountains. These latter were pursued by the mounted men under Captains Slack and St. Vrain, who killed fifty-one of them, only two or three escaping.[15]

The American loss at the battle of Taos Pueblo was seven killed and forty-five wounded, many of whom died later. Out of the estimated six or seven hundred rebels who participated in the fighting, one hundred fifty-four were killed, including Pablo Chavis, one of the leaders of the revolt. An unknown number of Indians and Mexicans were wounded.[16]

The following day, the Indian residents of Taos Pueblo sued for peace. Colonel Price agreed, provided that Tomacito, one of the two primary organizers of the revolt, be surrendered to the Americans. As it turned out, both of the instigators, Tomacito and Montoya, were captured. Dick Wootton participated in the battle, and his recollection of the fates of the two rebels was recalled in his biography in 1890.

El Tomacito, the Indian leader, was placed under guard, and we proposed to give him, along with the rest, a formal trial, but a dragoon by the name of Fitzgerald saved us the trouble. Fitzgerald was allowed to go into the room where the Indian was confined, along with others who wanted to take a look at him. The soldier looked at the savage a few minutes, and then quick as a flash, drew a pistol and shot him in the head, killing him instantly....The Indian deserved to be killed, and would have been hanged

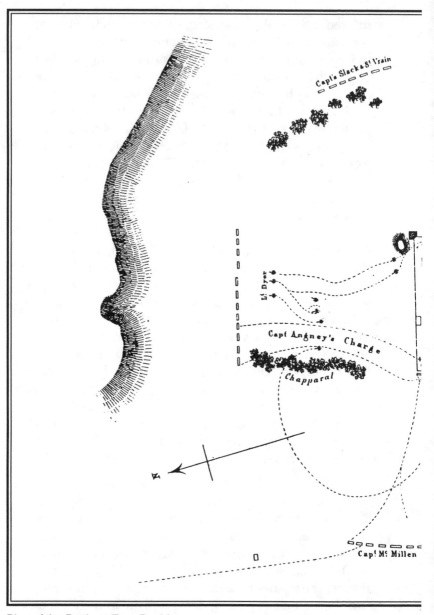

Plan of the Battle at Taos Pueblo
(From *Insurrection Against the Military Government in New Mexico and California, 1847 and 1848*)

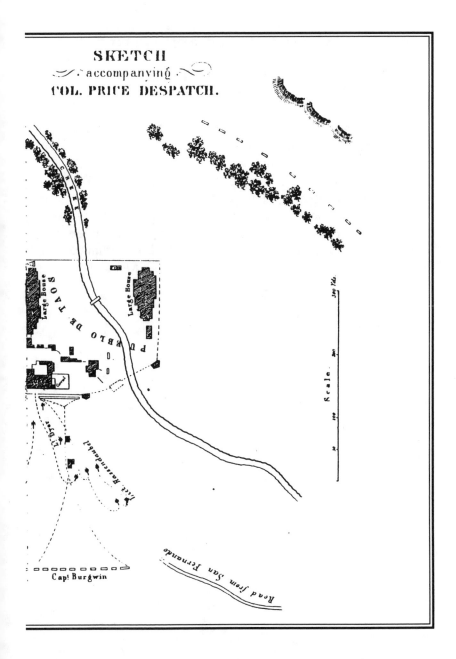

anyhow, but we objected to the informal manner of his taking off.

Pablo Montoya was tried and hanged, and twelve others were disposed of in the same way.[17]

With the successful conquest of Taos Pueblo by Colonel Price's troops, the revolt was all but over. The uprising had failed in its long-range objectives, but not without first taking the lives of scores of innocent people. The trials and executions of many of the revolt's conspirators were yet to come, but, for all intent and purposes, the decisive victory of the United States Army and the Missouri Mounted Volunteers at Taos Pueblo sealed the fate of the joint Mexican-Indian plan to permanently expel all Americans from New Mexico.

NOTES—CHAPTER FIVE

1. Although all of the official reports of the time refer to Captain Burgwin as "I.H.K." Burgwin, Francis B. Heitman, in his monumental *Historical Register and Dictionary of the United States Army* (Washington, D.C.: Government Printing Office, 1903) lists him as "John Henry K." Burgwin. Burgwin was born in North Carolina and graduated from the U.S. Military Academy in 1830.
2. *Insurrection*, pp. 8-13. Report of Colonel Sterling Price to the Adjutant General, February 15, 1846.
3. Ibid., p. 28.
4. Ibid., pp. 8-13.
5. Pierce, ed., *New Mexico Place Names*, pp. 148-149.
6. *Insurrection*, pp. 8-13. Report of Colonel Price.
7. Ibid.
8. Ibid.
9. Ibid.
10. Ibid., Letter of January 23, 1846, from Captain I.R. Hendley to Colonel Sterling Price, pp. 18-19.
11. Ibid., pp. 24-26, U.S. Proclamation.
12. Ibid., pp. 8-13, Report of Colonel Sterling Price.
13. Ibid.
14. Ibid., pp. 13-14, Letter from Woldemar Fischer to the Adjutant General, dated February 16, 1847.
15. Ibid., pp. 8-13, Report of Colonel Sterling Price, February 15, 1847.
16. Ibid.
17. Conard, *"Uncle Dick" Wootton*, pp. 184-186.

CHAPTER SIX

TRIAL AND EXECUTION

On February 15, 1847, Colonel Sterling Price sent a lengthy report to the adjutant general in Washington. In the message, he gave a careful and detailed accounting of his and his army's activities since they left Santa Fe in January to quell the revolt at Taos. Price was proud of the men under his command, and he proclaimed:

> In the battles of Cañada, Embudo, and Pueblo de Taos, the officers and men behaved admirabley [sic]. Where all conducted themselves gallantly, I consider it improper to distinguish individuals, as such discrimination might operate prejudicially against the just claims of others.[1]

When President Polk received the news of Price's victory, he placed great importance on the recent events in New Mexico. He recorded in his diary:

On yesterday official despatches [sic] were received from Col. Price, commanding at Santa Fé, announcing that a battle had been fought and a signal victory won by the troops under his command over the enemy. The number of troops engaged was comparatively small, but I consider this victory one of the most signal which has been gained during the war.[2]

Price took many captives during the battle at Taos Pueblo. When he prepared to march his soldiers back to the garrison at Santa Fe, leaving a contingent of them to man the garrison at Taos, he turned the prisoners over to local authorities for prosecution in the civilian court there. As the days of late winter turned into those of spring, Taos was engulfed with talk of the upcoming trials and their possible outcome. Although affairs in the town had returned to almost normal following the sound defeat of the rebels at the Pueblo, many residents were still concerned about the fates of their friends and neighbors at the hands of the American court system. As would soon be demonstrated, the trials of the captured revolutionaries were anticlimactic to the tragic events that had occurred in the Taos area during the previous few weeks. It took little imagination on anyone's part to accurately predict the outcome of the hearings, since the jury box was filled with either Americans or with Mexican loyalists.

Much of what is known today about the trials at Taos is derived from the book *Wah-to-Yah and the Taos Trail*, by Lewis H. Garrard, published in 1850. Garrard, not yet twenty years old, had joined a trading caravan at Westport Landing, Missouri, bound for Bent's Fort on the Arkansas. When he arrived at the fort, he stayed for several weeks, until he was recruited by William Bent to go to Taos to avenge the murder of Bent's late brother, Charles. Garrard attended most of the trials and subsequent hangings of the convicted rebels, and his account is the only unofficial record of the events as they occurred.

The court was presided over by Judge Charles H. Beaubien, the father of Narciso Beaubien, one of those murdered at Taos on January 19. Joab Houghton, a New York native and chief justice of the Territorial court system, served as an associate judge. The prosecuting attorney was Frank Blair. Both his assistant and the counsel for the defense were American army privates, selected because of their legal background. Charles Bent's old partner, Ceran St. Vrain, served as the official interpreter of the proceedings, and Charles's brother George was appointed foreman of the grand jury.

Charles Beaubien, chief judge at the Taos trials

(From *The History of the Military Occupation of the Territory of New Mexico from 1846 to 1851 by the Government of the United States*, by Ralph Emerson Twitchell)

The Circuit Court for the Northern District of New Mexico met in Taos from April 5 until April 24, 1847, and the trials for the revolutionaries were held from April 5 until April 13. Fifteen of the sixteen men charged with murder were convicted and sentenced to hang. Additionally, of the five men tried for treason, one was found guilty and sentenced to hang.[3] Punishment was swift. All of the sentenced men were hanged by May 7, 1846. Six of them were executed within two days of the sentencing. In 1926 Francis T. Cheetham, in a comprehensive article about the Taos trials, commented on the speed of the proceedings.

Ceran St. Vrain, partner of Charles Bent

(From *"Uncle Dick" Wootton*, by Howard L. Conard)

There was no talk about the law's delay here, for this court convicted a man of murder, for each and every working day of the term. Appeals were not much in favor in this court, for each homicide convict was hanged before a transcript could have been written.[4]

Lewis Garrard left a moving narrative of some of the court proceedings in his book. Of one of the trials, he commented:

Court assembled at nine o'clock. On entering the room, Judges Beaubien and Houghton were

Francis P. Blair, Jr., the American prosecutor at the Taos trials

(From *The History of the Military Occupation of the Territory of New Mexico from 1846 to 1851 by the Government of the United States,* by Ralph Emerson Twitchell)

occupying their official stations. After many dry pre-
liminaries, six prisoners were brought in—ill-favored,
half-scared, sullen fellows; and the jury of Mexicans
and Americans...being empaneled, the trial commenced....

When the witnesses (Mexican) touched their lips to
the Bible, on taking the oath, it was with such a combination of reverential awe for the book and the fear of
los Americanos that I could not repress a smile. The poor
things were as much frightened as the prisoners at
the bar.[5]

Garrard, while sympathizing with the families of those
Americans and Mexicans who were massacred by the rebels
during the assaults on Taos, Turley's Mill, Rio Colorado, and
Mora, gives the distinct impression in his narrative that he
was equally as sympathetic with the culprits, who after all,
were only defending their homeland. Garrard's scathing
words leave no doubt that he clearly appreciated and under-
stood both sides of the issue. His remarks relative to the
treason charge against one of the accused were especially
poignant.

It certainly did appear to be a great assumption on
the part of the Americans to conquer a country and
then arraign the revolting inhabitants for treason.
American judges sat on the bench, New Mexicans and
Americans filled the jury box, and an American
soldiery guarded the halls. Verily, a strange mixture of
violence and justice—a strange middle ground between the martial and common law.[6]

During this particular trial, the outcome was practically
guaranteed. Garrard continues his narrative:

After an absence of a few minutes, the jury returned with a verdict of 'guilty in the first degree'

—five for murder, one for treason. Treason, indeed! What did the poor devil know about his new allegiance? But so it was; and, as the jail was overstocked with others awaiting trial, it was deemed expedient to hasten the execution, and the culprits were sentenced to be hung on the following Friday—hangman's day. When the concluding words *'muerto, muerto, muerto'*— 'dead, dead, dead'—were pronounced by Judge Beaubien in his solemn and impressive manner, the painful stillness that reigned in the courtroom and the subdued grief manifested by a few bystanders were noticed not without an inward sympathy. The poor wretches sat with immovable features; but I fancied that under the assumed looks of apathetic indifference could be read the deepest anguish. When remanded to the jail till the day of execution, they drew their *sarapes* more closely around them and accompanied the armed guard. I left the room, sick at heart. Justice! Out upon the word, when its distorted meaning is the warrant for murdering those who defend to the last their country and their homes.[7]

Young Lewis Garrard was not the only person troubled by the introduction into the trial of "treason" charges against several of the rebels by American authorities. He wondered how a person who was conquered in war could be tried for treason against the conquering country. Unknown to Garrard and probably the rest of the crowd in the courtroom, the problem had it origins during the previous fall in the promulgation of "Kearny's Code," the set of laws written by Colonel Alexander Doniphan and Private Willard Hall of the 1st Missouri Regiment of Volunteers.

Members of the U.S. House of Representatives had questioned President Polk in December 1846, after a copy of

Kearny's Code was received in Washington. They wanted full information regarding any steps the United States had taken to establish civil government in New Mexico. President Polk responded that Kearny's Code had been received in Washington the previous month, but that it had only recently been brought to his attention. Polk explained the Code as follows:

> It is declared on its face to be a temporary govern-ment of the said territory, but there are portions of it which purport to 'establish and organize' a permanent Territorial government of the United States over the Territory and to impart to its inhabitants political rights, which, under the Constitution of the United States, can be enjoyed permanently only by citizens of the United States. These have not been 'approved and recognized' by me. Such organized regulations as have been established in any of the conquered ter-ritories for the security of our conquest, for the preservation of order, for the protection of the rights of the inhabitants, and for depriving the enemy of the advantages of these territories while the military pos-session of them by the forces of the United States continues, will be recognized and approved.[8]

Defending Kearny, Polk ended his reply by stating that:

> ...if any excess of power has been exercised, the departure has been the offspring of a patriotic desire to give to the inhabitants the privileges and immuni-ties so cherished by the people of our own country, and which they believed calculated to improve their condition and promote their prosperity. Any such excess has resulted in practically no injury, but can and will be early corrected in a manner to alienate as little as possible the good feelings of the inhabitants of the conquered territory.[9]

On January 11, 1847, just days after President Polk's encounter with Congress, Secretary of State William L. Marcy, following instructions from Polk himself, dispatched a message to Kearny mildly rebuking him for overstepping his authority. Marcy explained that Kearny did not have the authority to confer citizenship on the inhabitants of the newly occupied territory of New Mexico, stating that this privilege could only be granted by the United States Congress. Of course, by then, Kearny had already departed for California, but his Code continued to be the only version of American law in New Mexico.[10]

American prosecutors at the Taos trials, in keeping with their interpretation of the Kearny Code and their erroneous assumption that the newly conquered Mexican population was automatically bestowed with American citizenship, believed that treason was a reasonable charge to be lodged against some of the more recalcitrant revolutionaries. As affairs turned out, the treason charges were illegal on the premise that one cannot commit treason against a country of which he is not a citizen. A ruling from the United States Supreme Court on another case with its roots in the Mexican War underlined the illegality of some of the Taos proceedings as far as the treason charges were concerned. Justice Roger B. Taney wrote his opinion that:

> The relation in which the conquered territory stood to the United States while it was occupied by their arms did not depend on the laws of nations but upon our own constitution and acts of Congress.... The inhabitants were still foreigners and enemies, and owed to the United States nothing more than submission and obedience, sometimes called temporary allegiance, which is due from a conquered enemy when he surrenders to a force which he is unable to resist.[11]

Unfortunately, for one of those accused of treason at the Taos trials of early 1847, Justice Taney's ruling came a couple of years too late.

During the summer of 1848, after the Taos trials had been over for more than a year, President Polk was still being haunted by the treason issue. A congressional resolution was sent to the president asking him if the charge of treason against Mexican nationals during the aftermath of the revolt had resulted in execution. Polk replied on July 24, that:

> It appears that after the territory in question was in the occupancy of our Army, some of the conquered Mexican inhabitants, who had at first submitted to our authority, broke out in open insurrection, murdering our soldiers and citizens and committing other atrocious crimes. Some of the principal offenders who were apprehended were tried and condemned by a tribunal invested with civil and criminal jurisdiction, which had been established in the conquered country by the military officer in command. That the offenders deserved the punishment inflicted upon them there is no reason to doubt, and the error in the proceedings against them consisted in designating and describing their crimes as 'treason against the United States.' This error was pointed out, and its recurrence thereby prevented, by the Secretary of War, in a dispatch to the officer in command in New Mexico, dated on the 26th day of June, 1847.[12]

On April 7 and 8, during which time five Indians and four Mexicans were convicted of murder and sentenced to hang on April 30, Charles Bent's widow; his sister-in-law, Mrs. Kit Carson; and Mrs. Thomas Boggs attended the proceedings. Lewis H. Garrard was there and reported the following:

In the courtroom, on the occasion of the trial of the...nine prisoners, were Senora Bent, the late governor's wife and Senora Boggs, giving their evidence in regard to the massacre, of which they were eye-witnesses. Senora Bent was quite handsome; a few years since, she must have been a beautiful woman.... The other lady, though not so agreeable in appearance, was much younger. The wife of the renowned mountaineer Kit Carson also was in attendance.... The dress and manners of the three ladies bespoke a greater degree of refinement than usual.

The courtroom was a small, oblong apartment, dimly lighted by two narrow windows; a thin railing kept the bystanders from contact with the functionaries. The prisoners faced the judges, and the three witnesses (Senoras Bent, Boggs, and Carson) were close to them on a bench by the wall. When Mrs. Bent gave in her testimony, the eyes of the culprits were fixed sternly upon her; on pointing out the Indian who killed the Governor, not a muscle of the chief's face twitched or betrayed agitation, though he was aware her evidence unmistakenly sealed his death warrant—he sat with lips gently closed, eyes earnestly centered on her, without a show of malice or hatred—an almost sublime spectacle of Indian fortitude and of the severe mastery to which the emotions can be subjected. Truly, it was a noble example of Indian stoicism.[13]

And so, one by one, the accused leaders of the Taos Revolt of 1847 were sentenced by an overwhelmingly pro-American court and jury. The only thing left now was the actual prosecution of the imposed sentences.

If neither the speed nor the results of the trials surprised anyone in Taos, then neither should have the alacrity with which the Americans pursued the executions of those convicted. Hangings were held on April 9, April 30, and May 7. During the latter executions, the sheriff couldn't find enough rope and had to borrow several rawhide lariats from Lewis Garrard and his friends and some picket cords from a teamster. Garrard helped soap the makeshift leather lariats to make them softer, then went to the sheriff's office and observed the prisoners. "These men were the condemned," he commented. "In two short hours, they hung lifeless on the gallows...."[14]

The gallows, consisting of a scaffold of two upright posts with a crossbar connecting them, was situated about one hundred and fifty yards from the jailhouse. As the condemned approached their destiny, they "marched slowly, with down-cast eyes, arms tied behind, and bare heads, with the exception of white cotton caps stuck on the back part, to be pulled over the face as the last ceremony."[15]

The army took no chances. On the roof of the jail, soldiers aimed the mountain howitzer that had been used in the battle at the Taos Pueblo at the gallows. One man stood over the fuse with a lighted match in his hand. Two hundred thirty soldiers marched down the street in front of jail in a show of force. The sheriff and his assistant placed the nooses around the six prisoners' necks as officials balanced the men on a board that stretched across a wagon drawn by two mules.

Garrard watched as the proceeding drew to a close. In his book, he later wrote:

> ...succeeding a few moments of intense expectation, the heart-wrung victims said a few words to their people.
> But one said that they had committed murder and deserved death. In their brief, but earnest appeals, which I could but imperfectly comprehend, the words

"mi padre, mi madre"—"my father, my mother"—could be distinguished. The one sentenced for treason showed a spirit of martyrdom worthy to the cause for which he died—the liberty of his country; and, instead of the cringing, contemptible recantation of the others, his speech was firm asseverations of his own innocence, the unjustness of his trial, and the arbitrary conduct of his murderers.[16]

The command was at last given. The mules struggled to pull the combined weight of the wagon and the six men poised on its platform. "Bidding each other *'adios,'* with a hope of meeting in Heaven,"[17] the six accused swayed back and forth in the dry, gentle breeze. After the men had swung lifelessly for forty minutes, they were finally cut down. The military guard was dismissed, and the sad spectators slowly returned to their homes. Weeping relatives claimed the bodies, which Garrard helped take down from the scaffold. It was "a most unpleasant business, too, for the cold, clammy skins and dead weight were revolting to the touch...," he wrote.[18]

The repulsive task at hand now done, Garrard and his friends marched off to the local *cantina* and lost themselves in drink. It was all in a day's work, and after all, he kept telling himself, the guilty ones had been fairly tried and sentenced. As he wrote later, "Who *would* blame a man for making a temporary sacrifice of himself on Bacchus, on such an occasion...?"[19]

NOTES—CHAPTER SIX

1. *Insurrection*, p. 13.
2. Nevins, ed., Polk: *The Diary of a President*, pp. 218-219.
3. Francis T. Cheetham, "The First Term of the American Court in Taos, New Mexico," in *New Mexico Historical Review*, Vol. 1, No. 1, January, 1926, p. 27.
4. Ibid.
5. Lewis H. Garrard, *Wah-To-Yah and the Taos Trail* (Norman: University of Oklahoma Press, 1955), pp. 171-172.
6. Ibid., p. 172.
7. Ibid., pp. 172-173.
8. Polk, *Occupation of Mexican Territory*, p. 2.
9. Ibid.
10. Sister Mary Loyola, "The American Occupation of New Mexico, 1821-1852," in *New Mexico Historical Review*, Vol. 15, No. 3, July, 1939, p. 230.
11. Ibid., p. 231, note 3.
12. Message of President Polk, July 24, 1848, quoted in Twitchell, *The Military Occupation of New Mexico*, p. 144.
13. Garrard, *Wah-To-Yah*, pp. 181-182.
14. Ibid., p. 194.
15. Ibid., p. 196.
16. Ibid., p. 197.
17. Ibid.
18. Ibid., p. 198.
19. Ibid., p. 199.

EPILOGUE

Although the Taos Revolt "officially" ended when the last insurgents were hanged in Taos on May 7, 1847, sporadic fighting between Mexican and Indian rebels and the American army continued into the summer. In his July report to the adjutant general, Colonel Sterling Price, writing from Santa Fe, reported that:

> Since the insurrection of January and February last, a body of Mexicans and Indians, embodied for predatory purposes, have been very annoying along the line of eastern settlements of this Territory, where many of our grazing camps were established.[1]

Price advised Washington that on May 20, Captain Robinson's camp of Missouri Mounted Volunteers was attacked. The marauders made off with about two hundred horses and mules, and three soldiers were wounded, one of them fatally. When Major D.B. Edmonson, commander at Las Vegas, received information of the attack on Captain Robinson, he formed a detachment and marched at once in search of the rebels. On June 26 he found them in a deep canyon of the Canadian River. After sporatic fighting, his men failed to recover the horses and mules. The next day Lieutenant R.T. Brown of the Second Missouri Mounted Volunteers located the animals at Las Vallas, a small village located fifteen

Epilogue

The American Army attack on Las Vallas

(From *The History of the Military Occupation of the Territory of New Mexico from 1846 to 1851 by the Government of the United States*, by Ralph Emerson Twitchell)

miles south of Las Vegas. When he and his two companions attempted to reclaim the animals, the rebels fell upon them and killed all three men. Upon receipt of the information about the Brown massacre, Major Edmonson marched on Las Vallas, surprised its inhabitants, killed several, and took forty prisoners.

Captain Morin's company of Missouri Mounted Volunteers was set upon by rebels on July 6 while on grazing detail. Lieutenant Larkin and four other men were killed and nine more wounded. All of the horses and other equipment belonging to the Americans were stolen. Lieutenant Colonel Willock, commander at Taos, attempted to overtake the raiders, but failed. An exasperated Price added in his letter of July 20 to the adjutant general that "rumors of insurrections are rife..."[2]

Although Colonel Price had ample reason to be pessimistic about affairs in the region, his perception of the situation was rather one-sided. From the Mexican and local Indian standpoint, the new American government had not lived up to a very important promise made to them by General Kearny. Practically everywhere that the general spoke the previous year when he peacefully occupied New Mexico, he had vowed to his listeners American protection from raids by the warring Navajo tribe, among others. However, on only one occasion of record had the American military establishment attempted to tame the Navajos.

Colonel Alexander Doniphan, the commander of the First Missouri Mounted Volunteers, had left Santa Fe in late October, 1846, to penetrate deep into Navajo country and to attempt to treaty with that powerful tribe and end its continuous raids on the local population of Mexican farmers and villagers. Doniphan split his command into three elements and personally led one of them up the Rio Puerco to its headwaters. Major William Gilpin took two hundred troopers and, from Abiquiu, marched up the Rio Chama, across the Continental Divide, to the valley of the San Juan River. Captain John W. Reid and thirty soldiers marched cross-country straight into Navajo territory. By late November, about five hundred Navajos had assembled at Ojo del Oso in the heart of their homeland to hear what the Americans had to say.

The Navajos' spokesman was a young chief named Sarcilla Largo. He promptly told Doniphan that "he was gratified to learn the views of the Americans," adding that "he admired their spirit and enterprise, but detested the Mexicans." When Doniphan explained to him that the Mexicans had surrendered to the Americans and that the entire region was now under American rule, Sarcilla Largo replied,

> Americans! you have a strange cause of war against the Navajos. We have waged war against New Mexicans for several years. We have plundered their

Colonel Doniphan treating with Sarcilla Largo
(From *The History of the Military Occupation of the Territory of New Mexico from 1846 to 1851 by the Government of the United States,* by Ralph Emerson Twitchell)

villages and killed many of their people, and made many prisoners. We had just cause for all this. You have lately commenced a war against the same people. You are powerful. You have great guns and many brave soldiers. You have therefore conquered them, the very thing we have been attempting to do for so many years. You now turn upon us for attempting to do what you have done yourselves. We cannot see why you have cause of quarrel with us for fighting the New Mexicans on the west, while you do the same thing on the east. Look how matters stand. This is our war. We have more right to complain of you interfering in our war, than you have to quarrel with us for continuing a war we had begun long before you got here. If you will act justly, you will allow us to settle our own differences.[3]

When Colonel Doniphan explained to the Navajos that any war against the New Mexicans would now be war against the United States, the treaty was signed on November 22, 1846. Among other things, it declared a "firm and lasting peace and amity...between the American people and the Navajo tribe of Indians."[4]

This important treaty notwithstanding, the Navajos apparently continued to make trouble after the signing. According to a letter dated March 26, 1847 and written by Donaciano Vigil, the Mexican loyalist who had assumed the territory's governorship after Charles Bent was murdered, little had been done to allay the natives' fears of Navajo depredations. In a message to Secretary of State James Buchanan, Vigil related that Colonel Price had:

...received a deputation of principal men from the Navajo Indians, from whom he exacted a promise that all the prisoners and stock taken in their late marauding expeditions against the settlements of the southern district should be restored by the end of the present month.

I have no confidence of the fulfillment of the promise indeed, these Indians continue to commit daily outrage in the disregard of their promise. I hope measures will be immediately taken by the officer in command here to compel not only a restitution of property and prisoners, but to secure for the future respect for our arms and Government, and a lasting submission on the part of these turbulent savages. The interest and prosperity of the Territory urgently demands it.

In the late attacks of these Indians many citizens have been deprived of their all, and unless something be speedily done to prevent further depredations, the native citizens will have just cause to complain that the promises made to them by Brigadier-General Kearny, to the effect that they should be protected against these Indians, their ancient enemies, has been shamefully violated and disregarded.[5]

The lack of manpower also posed a serious problem to American authorities in Santa Fe. Enlistments were ending for many of the volunteers, and it was difficult to obtain replacements. Governor Vigil urged Secretary Buchanan to replace the volunteer force with regular troops as soon as possible, citing reasons of "greater economy, expediency, and efficiency."[6] Colonel Price, in his July letter to the adjutant general, confirmed Vigil's apprehensions about a volunteer army in which many of its soldiers' enlistments had terminated. He stated to his superior that, "The forces under my command are now so much diminished by the departure of the companies whose terms of service have expired, that I consider it necessary to concentrate my whole command at this city...."[7]

Colonel Price had other worries on his mind. Despite the recent victory over the Indians and Mexicans at Taos, he continued to be concerned about his army's position, so remotely located in enemy—albeit American—territory, with little hope of relief. The United States was still at war with Mexico, and regardless of the presence of American forces in the region, many natives still maintained a fierce loyalty to Mexico. Price cautioned the adjutant general that:

> ...it is said that a large force is approaching from the direction of Chihuahua. I am unable to determine whether these rumors are true or false, but it is certain that the New Mexicans entertain deadly hatred against Americans, and that they will cut off small parties of the latter whenever they think they can escape detection....[8]

As future events would soon prove, Colonel Price had worried needlessly about an invasion of New Mexico. Less than sixty days after he expressed his concerns to the adjutant general, American forces under General Winfield Scott captured Mexico City, thus all but ending the war with Mexico. On February 2, 1848, the Treaty of Guadalupe Hidalgo was signed between the two powers and ratified by the United States Senate the following month.

The ratification of the Treaty of Guadalupe Hidalgo made official what neither General Kearny's proclamations to the New Mexicans in the late summer of 1846 nor two years of fighting between the United States and Mexico could. At last, New Mexico, California, and a large portion of today's Southwest were formally designated a part of the United States. The inevitable had finally occurred, and the wanton bloodshed by both factions in Taos and the surrounding countryside in January 1847 turned out to be all for naught.

NOTES—EPILOGUE

1. *Insurrection*, pp. 20-21.
2. Ibid., p. 21.
3. Hughes, *Doniphan's Expedition*, p. 187.
4. Ibid., p. 188.
5. *Insurrection*, p. 31.
6. Ibid., p. 32.
7. Ibid., p. 21.
8. Ibid.

Appendixes

Who Was Who in the Taos Revolt and the American Occupation of New Mexico

James W. Abert (1820-1897)
A son of the Chief of Topographical Engineers, James W. Abert was destined for a military life. Originally ordered to accompany Kearny's Army of the West to Santa Fe, young Abert took ill on the way and stayed behind at Bent's Fort to recover. When he was well enough to travel, he proceeded on to New Mexico, where he surveyed the countryside, made an accurate map of the region, and took copious notes about the natural resources of the area. After the Mexican War, Abert taught at West Point and served in the Union Army during the Civil War. Picking up his teaching career again after the War, he died in Kentucky.

John D. Albert (1806-1899)

Albert, the mountain man who escaped the massacre at Turley's Mill to bring word of the slaughter to other mountain men gathered at the site of Pueblo, Colorado, was born in Hagerstown, Maryland. He eventually settled at Walsenberg, Colorado, where he spent the rest of his life.

Diego Archuleta (1814-1884)

Diego Archuleta was born in New Mexico and after adulthood, followed a military career. He participated in the defense of New Mexico during the Texan-Santa Fe Expedition of 1841. When the American army marched across the Santa Fe Trail in late 1846 to occupy New Mexico, Archuleta was second in command in the New Mexican army and reported directly to Governor Armijo. The American envoy to Armijo, James Magoffin, in secret talks in Santa Fe in late 1846, led Armijo to believe that the western bank of the Rio Grande would not be occupied by the United States. When, in fact, General Kearny publicly announced the conquest of all of New Mexico, Archuleta engineered an abortive attempt to overthrow American authorities. Archuleta later took the oath of allegiance to the United States and served his adopted country as Indian agent, member of the legislative assembly, and candidate for the U.S. Congress. His funeral procession of more than 2,500 mourners was one of the largest ever witnessed in Santa Fe.

Manuel Armijo (?—1853)

Don Manuel Armijo, the Mexican governor of New Mexico at the time the American army occupied Santa Fe in August 1846, was born of poor parentage at an unknown date in New Mexico. Climbing through the ranks of government, Armijo finally, through political intrigue, became governor in 1827. He was largely responsible for the persecution of Americans involved in the Texan-Santa Fe Expedition of 1841, sending most of them to prison in Mexico City. Twice more, he served as governor of New Mexico, from 1837 to 1844 and from

1845 to 1846, when he was ousted by the American occupation. Described by the English writer Ruxton as "a mountain of fat," Armijo, nevertheless, cut a dashing figure as a young man. The former governor died, a rejected and disappointed man, on December 9, 1853. Out of respect for the one-time official, the New Mexico Territorial Assembly adjourned its session of December 13, 1853.

Charles H. Beaubien (1800-1864)
Charles Beaubien arrived in New Mexico in 1824. By 1827 he was a permanent resident of Taos, becoming a Mexican citizen two years later. He acquired a huge land grant from the Mexican government and established himself as a well-to-do landowner. His son, Narciso, was one of those killed by Mexicans and Indians at Taos on the morning of January 19, 1847. Charles Beaubien sat as the presiding judge during the trials in Taos for the captured revolutionaries.

Charles Bent (1799-1847)
Charles Bent, the eldest of the famous Bent brothers—the others were William, George, and Robert—was born in Charleston, Virginia (now West Virginia). When he was six years old, Bent moved to St. Louis with his family, and there, in the town that was the gateway to the West, he grew to manhood, amid the sights and sounds of the trapper and trader communities. Young Bent tried his hand at fur trapping with the Missouri Fur Company, but favored the Southwest trade instead. He became one of the leading American merchants to ply the Santa Fe Trail to New Mexico. Later, after building Bent's Fort with his brother William and his partner Ceran St. Vrain, Charles moved to Taos, leaving the day-to-day business at the fort to William. In 1846 he was appointed as the first American civil governor of New Mexico by General Stephen Watts Kearny, a position he held but a brief time. On January 19, 1847, in his hometown of Taos, Bent and several other Americans and Mexicans with American sympathies

were murdered in a revolt that, before it was over, spread to much of north-central New Mexico.

Francis P. Blair, Jr. (1821-1875)

Francis Blair was born in Lexington, Kentucky, the son of Frank Blair, the editor of the Washington *Globe* and the president's "mouth-piece" during Andrew Jackson's administration. Francis was at Bent's Fort in mid-1846, when Colonel Stephen Watts Kearny's Army of the West arrived. He accompanied the army to Santa Fe, where he assisted Colonel Doniphan and others in the creation of the *Kearny Code*. Before he left for California, Kearny appointed young Blair to the position of United States attorney, the job he held when he brought indictments against a number of Taos Indians and Mexicans after the Taos Revolt. Blair left New Mexico in late 1847 and returned to Missouri, and in 1852 he was elected to the legislature. He served as a Union major general during the Civil War and saw action at Vicksburg. In 1868 he was the Democratic Party's unsuccessful nominee for vice president and later served as U.S. senator from Missouri.

Manuel Antonio Chaves (1818-?)

Manuel Chaves was born of well-to-do parents near Albuquerque. As a young man, he fought against the marauding Navajos. In 1841, when the participants of the Texan-Santa Fe Expedition were poised to invade New Mexico, he and Diego Archuleta were ordered to capture a large party of the Texans. Later, Chaves was an officer at the so-called defense of Apache Pass, when Governor Armijo fled south. Chaves was arrested by Colonel Sterling Price, when it became suspected that he was involved in a plot to overthrow the newly installed American government. When he was asked in prison if he was, indeed, part of the scheme, Chaves reportedly replied, "Captain, be kind enough to take my compliments to General Price and say that he has nothing to fear from me now. When Armijo disbanded the volunteer army at Canoncito, I gave up all hope of being of any service to my country at this time, and my record as a man will show that I am not at all likely to sympathize with any movement to murder people in cold blood. Tell him also that if the time ever comes when I can be of any service to my own country, General Price will find me in the front ranks." He was charged with treason, but was acquitted. When Governor Bent was murdered soon afterwards, Chaves marched on Taos Pueblo as an enlisted man with the Americans. After the Mexican War, Chaves served with his new American countrymen against the Utes and the Apaches. When the Civil War broke out, he was offered a commission in the Confederate army, but chose to remain a Union loyalist, serving in the New Mexico Volunteer Infantry.

Philip St. George Cooke (1809-1895)
Philip St. George Cooke was born in Leesburg, Virginia, and graduated from West Point in 1827. He served with the 6th Infantry and fought in the Black Hawk War of 1832. Transferring to the 1st Dragoons, he was promoted to captain in 1835. General Stephen Watts Kearny, the commander of the Army of the West, placed Cooke in charge of the Mormon Battalion, which marched to California soon after Kearny left Santa Fe in late 1846. Although practically all of his family was pro-Southern, Cooke remained in the Union army when the Civil War broke out. After the War, he saw service again in the West, retiring in 1873 as a brigadier general, breveted to major general. His book *The Conquest of New Mexico and California* is a good source of information about American military activity in the region during the Mexican War.

Alexander W. Doniphan (1808-1887)
Alexander Doniphan was born in Mason County, Kentucky. As a youth, he moved to Missouri, the outskirts of civilization at the time. He was elected colonel and commander of the 1st Missouri Mounted Volunteers which accompanied Colonel Kearny's Army of the West from Fort Leavenworth to Santa Fe in the summer of 1846. After Colonel Sterling Price arrived

in Santa Fe with a second regiment of Missourians, Doniphan reported to General Jonathan Wool in Chihuahua, where his command became part of Wool's army. After the Mexican War, Doniphan returned to Missouri where he pursued civil matters. Although he personally opposed slavery, he took no active part in the Civil War. He died at Richmond, Missouri.

William Helmsley Emory (1811-1887)
Colonel Stephen Watts Kearny's chief topographical engineer was Lieutenant William H. Emory. Born in Maryland, Emory graduated from West Point in 1831. It is from Emory's outstanding document, *Notes of a Military Reconnoissance* that much present-day knowledge about the American conquest of New Mexico is derived. After the Mexican War, Emory was active in the railroad surveys which defined the routes of the railroad to the Pacific. During the Civil War, Emory served in the Union army and attained the rank of brevet major general. He retired from active duty as a full brigadier general.

Thomas (Broken Hand) Fitzpatrick (1799-1854)
Fitzpatrick was born in Ireland, but after his arrival in the United States, he became, according to one authority, "one of the three or four greatest mountain men and Indian managers." He was with General William Ashley during the battle at the Arikara villages in 1823. In 1841 Fitzpatrick quit the fur trade and took up scouting for emigrant parties and the military. He was guide for Colonel Kearny's Army of the West from Fort Leavenworth to Santa Fe and beyond. He was later appointed Indian Agent for the Upper Platte and Arkansas rivers region and was successful in maintaining peace between the southern Plains tribes and the ever-westward-moving Americans. Called "Broken Hand" because of his crippled left hand caused by a firearms accident, Fitzpatrick was a legend in his own time.

Lewis H. Garrard (1829-1887)
Lewis H. Garrard, sometimes known as Hector Lewis Garrard, was born in Cincinnati, Ohio. As a youth, he left his

home to visit the Rocky Mountains. From Westport Landing, in Missouri, Garrard joined a caravan under the leadership of Ceran St. Vrain, destined for Bent's Fort. Garrard spent several months at the fort and then joined a party recruited by William Bent to avenge the murder in Taos of Bent's brother Charles. After the Taos trials (Garrard was the only eyewitness to the trials to leave an account), he returned to the East and studied medicine. In later years, Garrard was one of the earliest settlers in southeastern Minnesota, where he became a prominent physician. Garrard died in Cincinnati.

Stephen Watts Kearny (1794-1847)
Colonel (later brigadier general) Stephen Watts Kearny was born in New Jersey. He served in the War of 1812, emerging from the conflict as a captain. Sent to the frontier, Kearny was promoted to lieutenant colonel of the 1st United States Dragoons in 1833, succeeding to the command of the regiment in 1836, with the rank of colonel. From that point on, he assumed the role of effective leader of the United States cavalry, the unit which eventually evolved from the dragoons. Kearny served many years on the Great Plains, culminating in his assignment as commander of the Army of the West. After he left New Mexico for California in late 1846, he conquered and occupied Los Angeles on January 10, 1847. Kearny returned to Fort Leavenworth in 1847, but died the following year in St. Louis from a disease he had contracted in Mexico.

Stephen Louis Lee (1808-1847)
Lee moved from his birthplace in Kentucky to New Mexico in 1824. He was a Taos-based trapper and trader and was appointed sheriff of Taos in 1846 by Governor Charles Bent. Lee was one of the Americans who, in addition to Bent, was murdered by Mexican and Indian rebels in Taos on January 19, 1847.

James Wiley Magoffin (1799-1868)
By the time he was twenty-six years old, Kentucky-born James W. Magoffin had already established himself as a leading

Santa Fe trader. He served as U.S. consul to Mexico for several years. This tenure, added to his familiarity with New Mexico through his many years as a trader, made Magoffin a prime candidate to send ahead of Colonel Kearny's army to try to persuade Governor Armijo to give up New Mexico peacefully. Magoffin was later arrested as a spy in Mexico, but his popularity with the people saved him from execution. When Magoffin returned to the United States, he attempted to collect $50,000 from the government for services rendered in New Mexico and Mexico. The claim was eventually settled for $30,000. He sided with the Confederacy during the Civil War, and one of his sons was killed during the conflict. Magoffin died in San Antonio and was buried locally.

Antonio Jose Martinez (1793-1867)
Some authorities maintain that Father Martinez played a large role in the Taos Revolt that witnessed the murders of Governor Charles Bent and several others. Martinez was born in Rio Arriba County, New Mexico. He detested the presence of Americans in New Mexico, and according to Ralph Emerson Twitchell, New Mexico's eminent historian, his home "was generally regarded as the headquarters for the insurrectionists prior to the uprising and until after the assassination of Governor Bent. His power over his parishioners was absolute and his hatred of Americans and American institutions was recognized by all." Father Martinez died in Taos and is buried there.

Nicolas Pino (?-1896) and Miguel E. Pino (?-?)
The Pino brothers, Nicolas and Miguel, were involved in the December 1846 plot to overthrow the Americans in Santa Fe. After this scheme fell through, both brothers took the oath of allegiance to the United States and served their new country in a variety of roles. Nicolas fought with the Americans at Taos Pueblo during the fierce fighting there in January 1847. Both brothers served as officers of New Mexico volunteer troops

during the Civil War, and both served in a variety of public offices.

James K. Polk (1795-1849)

James K. Polk was virtually unknown when he was nominated for the presidency in 1844. Born in North Carolina, he moved to Tennessee as a young man and practiced law in Columbia, a small town about forty miles south of Nashville. He later served in the U.S. House of Representatives for several years, four of them as speaker. That position notwithstanding, Polk's was still not exactly a household name like that of former President Martin van Buren, who was dumped at the convention in his favor, or of Henry Clay, the Whig nominee whom he defeated in the general election. When he became president in 1845, Polk endorsed the earlier moves by his predecessor, John Tyler, which would assure that the vast land comprising the Republic of Texas did, indeed, join the Union. When the annexation issue could not be resolved with Mexico peacefully, Polk recommended to Congress that war be declared. By the Mexican War's end, the United States government had acquired one-half million square miles of the present-day Southwest and California. This massive acquisition, coupled with the territory gained by his successful negotiation with Great Britain about the Oregon question, put Polk in the position of adding more real estate to the Union than any other president. But, his one term of office had taken its toll. Less than four months after leaving the presidency, Polk died at his home in Nashville.

Sterling Price (1809-1867)

Although born in Virginia, Sterling Price was a Missourian at heart. Price moved to the frontier across the Mississippi when he was twenty-one years old, and from that point on, he placed the welfare of Missouri above all else in his public life. Before he led the 2d Missouri Mounted Volunteers to Santa Fe in late 1846, Price had already served in the state legislature for three terms and in the U.S. Congress for one. After his

Mexican War service, Price was elected governor of Missouri in 1852. At the outbreak of the Civil War, he took up the flag of the Confederacy, spending most of his career in the trans-Mississippi theater. After the War, Major General Price spent time in exile in Mexico, but he eventually returned to Missouri where he died.

George Frederick Ruxton (1821-1848)
Ruxton was born in England, and after an enlistment with the British army in Canada, he went south and ended up in New Mexico, leaving the area just prior to the Taos Revolt of 1847. Ruxton was a prolific writer, and it is due to his observations that the latter days of the Rocky Mountain fur trade are so well documented. Theodore Roosevelt wrote that "No one was to equal him in his portrayal of the Rockies and their Mountain Men...." After the Mexican War, Ruxton returned to England where he worked on his books and articles about the American West. Later, he made another trip to the United States, but died in St. Louis before he could again see the land that he loved.

Ceran St. Vrain (1802-1870)
An American frontiersman of French descent, Ceran St. Vrain was born in Missouri. St. Vrain often visited Taos as a young man; in fact he frequented the town as early as 1825. Eventually, St. Vrain entered into partnership with Charles Bent, and the two traders established the Bent, St. Vrain Company, known throughout the southern Great Plains as the premier trading concern. St. Vrain played a pivotal role in the American attack on Taos Pueblo in January 1847. After the Mexican War, St. Vrain lived in the small village of Mora, New Mexico, where he died and is buried.

Tom Tate Tobin (1823-1904)
Tom Tobin and John Albert were the only two men to escape death during the massacre at Turley's Mill on January 19-20, 1847. From Turley's, Tobin went to Santa Fe to spread the word about the Mexican and Indian attack. After the Mexican

War, Tobin continued to trap and to serve as a scout. He outlived his friends by many years. Tobin is buried at Fort Garland, Colorado.

Simeon Turley (1806-1847)

Simeon Turley was born in Kentucky and migrated to Missouri around 1816. Moving to New Mexico in 1830, Turley settled at Arroyo Hondo, several miles north of Taos. He married a Mexican woman and was well accepted by his Mexican neighbors. His distillery soon became known for its fine whiskey, the forerunner of "Taos Lightning." Turley's rapport and friendship with the local citizenry proved to be his downfall in January 1847, when his compound was destroyed—and most of its defenders were killed—by rebel Mexicans and Indians.

Donaciano Vigil (1802-1877)

Donaciano Vigil was born in Santa Fe into a family of limited means. Receiving his education locally, Vigil gravitated toward the military and led several campaigns against the Navajos. He was serving on Governor Armijo's staff when the American army approached Santa Fe in late 1846. Shocked at Armijo's refusal to fight the Americans at Apache Pass, Vigil shifted his loyalties to the Americans. His cousin, Juan Bautista Vigil y Alarid, surrendered Santa Fe to Kearny and his troops. When Charles Bent was appointed governor of New Mexico, Donaciano Vigil was made the secretary of the territory. After Bent was murdered in Taos in January 1847, Vigil succeeded him and held the position until October 1848, when he was replaced by an American. He later served in a number of elective offices, including the New Mexico legislature. When Vigil died at Santa Fe, his funeral was attended by the largest crowd ever to assemble there.

Richens Lacy ("Uncle Dick") Wootton (1816-1893)

Dick Wootton was born in Virginia and moved west at a young age, later working for the Bent, St. Vrain Company. A self-proclaimed mountain man, Wootton operated in the

Colorado-New Mexico region for several years. Although a frequent visitor to Taos, Wootton was not present during the revolt in which his friend Charles Bent was murdered. Passages from his biography, *"Uncle Dick" Wootton*, indicate that he was familiar with the incident. He and several friends arrived at the Taos Pueblo in February 1847, in time to participate in the fighting there which ended the Taos Revolt. Wootton was later responsible for the construction of the toll road over Raton Pass on the Colorado-New Mexico border. He died at his home near Trinidad, Colorado.

APPENDIX B

A Chronology of Events Surrounding the Taos Revolt

1846

May 13　The United States declares war on Mexico almost three weeks after Mexican soldiers cross the Rio Grande and kill eleven American troopers.

May 13　Secretary of War William L. Marcy advises Colonel Stephen Watts Kearny, commander of the 1st Regiment of Dragoons at Fort Leavenworth, that war has been declared with Mexico. The adjutant general advises Kearny that a mounted force, probably commanded by him, will soon be organized and sent to New Mexico to occupy Santa Fe. Marcy also requests that Governor John C. Edwards of Missouri raise a regiment, consisting of eight companies of mounted volunteers and two companies of volunteer artillery.

May 14   Adjutant General Jones confirms to Colonel Kearny that he will command the army to be sent to New Mexico.

May 30   President James K. Polk and his advisors adopt the plan that Colonel Kearny will proceed to Santa Fe, and after the occupation of New Mexico is completed, that he will continue to California, weather permitting.

June 3   Secretary of War Marcy advises Kearny that a command will be created to conduct the occupation of New Mexico and California, and that he will be the senior officer. Marcy also tells Kearny about the raising of the Mormon Battalion.

June 18   All volunteer forces from Missouri have gathered at Fort Leavenworth. Alexander W. Doniphan, a well-known lawyer, is elected colonel and commander of the 1st Missouri Mounted Volunteers.

June 29   Colonel Kearny leaves Fort Leavenworth with his Army of the West, consisting of approximately 1,658 men.

Late   Elements of the Army of the West begin arriving at
July   Bent's Fort on the Arkansas River.

July 31   Colonel Kearny prepares a proclamation announcing the occupation of New Mexico by the American army to distribute to the Mexican populace as he proceeds to New Mexico.

Aug. 1   General Kearny dispatches James Wiley Magoffin, a well-known and respected Missouri trader, to Santa Fe to parley with Governor Armijo and to attempt to negotiate a peaceful surrender of Santa Fe and the rest of New Mexico.

Aug. 2   The Army of the West breaks camp at Bent's Fort and begins the final leg of its journey to Santa Fe.

Aug. 6   Lead elements of the Army of the West approach and ascend Raton Pass. The crossing is made with difficulty the next day.

Aug. 8   The New Mexican governor, Manuel Armijo, issues his own proclamation in which he urges his subjects to hear "the signal of alarm which must prepare us for battle."

Aug. 10   An escaped American from Taos reports to Colonel Kearny that Governor Armijo has assembled a large force of Mexicans and Indians to resist the Army of the West. Several Mexican civilians are captured and have on their persons copies of a call to arms issued by the prefect of Taos and based on Armijo's proclamation.

Aug. 12   James Magoffin, escorted by Captain Philip St. George Cooke, enters Santa Fe. Magoffin secretly meets with Governor Armijo and persuades him not to resist the American occupation. Magoffin leads Armijo's second-in-command, Diego Archuleta, to believe that the Americans have no interest in the west bank of the Rio Grande.

Aug. 13   Another American enters Kearny's camp with additional reports of native unrest and information that Governor Armijo is gathering a large army at Apache Canyon a few miles east of Santa Fe.

Aug. 14   As extra precautions are taken among the American troops, a letter from Armijo is received by Kearny exclaiming, "If you take the country, it will be because you prove strongest in battle...." Kearny's army camps on the outskirts of Vegas (today's Las Vegas).

Aug. 15   Colonel Kearny receives news that he has been promoted to brigadier general. He rides into Vegas and, from atop a roof of one of the buildings on the plaza, he reads the proclamation in which he claims New Mexico for the United States.

Aug. 16   The Army of the West rides into San Miguel. General Kearny makes a speech to the village's citizens similar to the one given at Vegas.

Aug. 17   Rumors reach the American camp that the Mexican soldiers at Apache Canyon under the command of Governor Armijo have fled.

Aug. 18   As Apache Canyon is approached by the Army of the West, its soldiers, totally unaware of the secret negotiations between Magoffin and Armijo, are ecstatic when they find that the enemy has fled. At noon, Kearny is approached by two Mexican officials who tell him the way to Santa Fe is clear and that the American army will meet no resistance. Advance elements of the army enter Santa Fe at three o'clock, with the remainder arriving at around six. As dusk approaches, the American colors are run up the flag staff in the plaza opposite the Governors' Palace.

Aug. 19   General Kearny assembles the citizens of Santa Fe in the Plaza and delivers an address similar to the ones given at Vegas and San Miguel. Former Lieutenant Governor Juan Bautista Vigil y Alarid makes a speech in which he accepts the United States occupation.

Aug. 22   General Kearny issues his proclamation to the people of Santa Fe. He leaves no doubt that it is the American plan to occupy all of New Mexico, including the west bank of the Rio Grande. Kearny sends a dispatch to General Jonathan E. Wool in Chihuahua that the occupation was accomplished peacefully and without bloodshed.

Aug. 23   Work begins on Fort Marcy, which is planned to protect Santa Fe from a height above the city.

Sept. 2   On the basis of a rumor that former Governor Armijo is approaching with an army to retake Santa Fe, General Kearny and a sizable force of dragoons head south out of Santa Fe to meet him and to survey the surrounding territory.

Sept. 4   With his army in the neighborhood of present-day Bernallilo, General Kearny learns that the reports about a Mexican buildup are false. He continues his tour.

Sept. 11   General Kearny and his dragoons return to Santa Fe.

Sept. 15   General Kearny sends a small party to Taos to reconnoiter the land and to determine the condition of the road connecting the village with Santa Fe.

Sept. 16   In a dispatch to the adjutant general in Washington, General Kearny assures army officials that everything is peaceful in Santa Fe.

Sept. 22   General Kearny appoints Charles Bent as the governor of New Mexico. Donaciano Vigil, a cousin of the former lieutenant governor, is named secretary of the territory. Kearny sends a copy of his *Laws of the Territory of New Mexico* to officials in Washington, D.C.

Sept. 25   General Kearny, with three hundred of his own 1st United States Dragoons, leaves Santa Fe for the second phase of his mission—to occupy California. Left behind in Santa Fe are Colonel Doniphan and his 1st Missouri Mounted Volunteers. A few scattered units of the 1st Dragoons also remain.

Dec.   During the month, army officials begin to receive reports of an intended revolt. The rumor mill has it that Governor Bent, newly arrived Colonel Sterling Price, and many other Americans are to be killed. Authorities act quickly and the revolution is aborted during the closing days of the month. Governor Bent issues a proclamation imploring Mexican residents to refrain from participating in revolutionary activities.

Dec. 26   Governor Bent dispatches details of the failed revolt to U.S. Secretary of State James Buchanan.

1847

Jan. 14   Governor Bent leaves Santa Fe for his home in Taos. With him are the new sheriff, Stephen Lee; the circuit attorney, James W. Leal; and a prefect, Cornelio Vigil.

Jan. 19   During the early morning hours, Governor Bent is awakened at his home, murdered, and his body mutilated by Mexican and Indian dissidents. The three companions with him on the trip to Taos are murdered as well, in addition to two other citizens, Narciso Beaubien and Pablo Jaramillo. Rebels at Arroyo Hondo, a few miles north of Taos, attack Simeon Turley's mill and distillery and, over a two-day period, kill all but two of the defenders. At Rio Colorado, revolutionaries kill two other mountain men, while at Mora, several traders are murdered by another group of rebels.

Jan. 20   News of the Taos Revolt reaches Colonel Sterling Price at Santa Fe. He immediately formulates plans to attack the rebels at Taos.

Jan. 21   Additional action at Mora results in the death of several more soldiers who are members of a grazing detail.

Jan. 22   Acting Governor Donaciano Vigil issues a proclamation from Santa Fe urging all citizens to cease their resistance to the American occupation.

Jan. 23   Colonel Price leaves Santa Fe with a contingent of 2d Missouri Mounted Volunteers. He heads for the revolutionaries' stronghold at Taos.

Jan. 24   Colonel Price and his small army successfully rout a much larger force of rebels at the village of Cañada.

Jan. 25   Captain I.R. Hendley and eighty soldiers march on Mora. Hendley is killed in the ensuing battle. Americans are forced to retreat when they are unable to dislodge the rebels from an old fort without artillery.

Jan. 27   Soon after leaving Cañada, Colonel Price's command is met by a large force of rebels near the village of Embudo. The Americans defeat the Mexicans.

Feb. 1   In retaliation for the death of Captain Hendley at Mora, Captain Morin levels the town with artillery fire.

Feb. 3   Colonel Price and his command reach Taos. Finding that the rebels are holed up in the Taos Pueblo about three miles north of town, they proceed there and begin to shell the Indian village. Nightfall cuts the action short, and the Americans retire for the evening.

Feb. 4   After several hours of heavy artillery fire, Colonel Price's men finally breach the thick walls of the Pueblo church. As rebels attempt to escape the village, they are cut down by Captain St. Vrain's volunteers. The battle at Taos Pueblo effectively ends the Taos Revolt.

Feb. 5   Leaders of the rebels sue for peace.

Feb. 7   The rebel Montoya is hanged at Taos.

Mar. 26   Governor Vigil, in a letter to Secretary of State James Buchanan, complains that General Kearny's promises of American protection from the hostile Navajos have not been forthcoming.

April 5   The trials for the imprisoned revolutionaries begin in Taos. The court is presided over by Judge Charles H. Beaubien, the father of one of the men killed in the Taos Revolt on January 19.

April 9   Execution of the Taos rebels begins.

April 13   The Taos trials end. The final tally: fifteen of the sixteen accused are convicted of murder and sentenced to hang. Of the five men tried for treason, one is found guilty and sentenced to hang.

April 30   More hangings take place in Taos.

May 7   The last of the executions of the Taos revolutionaries occurs.

May 20   Captain Robinson and his detachment of Missouri Mounted Volunteers are attacked near Mora. The Americans lose one man killed, two are wounded, and two hundred horses are stolen.

June 26   Major D.B. Edmonson, commander of the army contingent at Vegas, after a long pursuit, finds the attackers of Captain Robinson's grazing party on the Canadian River, but the Americans are unsuccessful in recapturing the horses.

June 27   Lieutenant R.T. Brown of the 2d Missouri Mounted Volunteers catches up with the stolen horses and the Mexicans who took them. Brown and two companions are killed. Major Edmonson later attacks the Mexican village where the horses were located and takes forty prisoners.

July 6   Captain Morin's company of Missouri Mounted Volunteers is attacked and five men are killed and nine wounded. All army property, including the horses, is stolen.

July 20   Colonel Sterling Price, in a letter to the adjutant general in Washington, reveals that "Rumors of insurrection are rife."

Sept. 14 General Winfield Scott captures Mexico City, thereby all but ending the Mexican War.

1848

Feb. 2   The Treaty of Guadalupe Hidalgo, officially ending the war, is signed between representatives of the United States and Mexico.

APPENDIX C

A List of Killed and Wounded in Battles

A list of American men killed and wounded at the battles of Canada, Embudo, and Pueblo de Taos fought during January and February 1847. From *Insurrection Against the Military Government in New Mexico and California, 1847 and 1848*, 56th Congress, 1st Session, Senate Document 442, Washington, D.C., 1900.

List of the killed and wounded at Cañada, Embudo, and Pueblo de Taos.

AT THE BATTLE OF CAÑADA, JANUARY 24, 1847.

Names	Rank	Company	Regiment and battalion	Remarks
Killed:				
Graham............	Private.........	Company B........	Infantry battalion	In employ quarter-master
G. Messersmith	Teamster......	Volunteered for the occasion.	........do.................	
Wounded:				
Irvine...............	First lieutenant	Company A........	........do.................	Acting adjutant battalion.
John Pace.......	Private.........	........do...............	........do.................	Slightly.
Caspers...........	First sergeant	B, mounted artillery	Lieutenant Dyer's detachment	Do.
Aulmon...........	Private.........	........do...............	........do.................	Severely.
Murphy...........	......do...........	C, artillery.........	........do.................	
Mezer..............	......do...........	B, artillery........	........do.................	

AT THE BATTLE OF EMBUDO, JANUARY 29, 1847.

Killed:				
Papin...............	Private.........	Santa Fe Volunteers.	Capt. St. Vrains's company.	
Wounded:				
Dick.................	(A negro)......	Governor Bent's.	Servant...............	Severely wounded.

AT PUEBLO DE TAOS, ON FEBRUARY 4, 1847.

Killed:				
Atkins..............	Teamster.......	Ammunition wagon.	Employ of quartermaster	
Wounded:				
Alfred L. .... Caldwell	First sergeant	K, Lieutenant White.	Second Regiment Missouri Volunteers.	Mortally wounded (since dead)
James Austin...	Private.........	........do...............	........do.................	Do.
James W. Jones	Third corprl.	........do...............	........do.................	Severely wounded.
Robert C. .... Bower	Private.........	A, Lieutenant E.W. Boone.	........do.................	Do.
Saml. Lewis.....	Private.........	M, Captain Halley.	Second Regiment Missouri Volunteers.	Severely wounded.

AT PUEBLO DE TAOS, ON FEBRUARY 4, 1847.

Names	Rank	Company	Regiment and battalion	Remarks
Wounded-Cont.				
T.G. West.........	First lieutenant	N, Captain Barbee	........do.................	Do.
I.H. Callaway...	Private...........	........do............	........do.................	Do.
John Nagel.......	........do...........	........do............	........do.................	Do.
John J. Sights...	........do...........	........do............	........do.................	Do.
Sam H. McMillan	Captain..........	D, Captain McMillan	........do.................	Do.
Henry Fender...	Private...........	........do............	........do.................	Dangerously wounded.
Geo. W. Johnson	........do...........	........do............	........do.................	Do.
Robt. Hewitt....	........do...........	........do............	........do.................	Slightly wounded.
Geo. W. Howser	........do...........	........do............	........do.................	Do.
Wm. Ducoing...	........do...........	........do............	........do.................	Do.
John Mansfield	Lieutenant....	L, Captain Slack	........do.................	Do.
Jacob Noon......	Private...........	........do............	........do.................	Severely wounded.
Wm. Gibbons...	........do...........	........do............	........do.................	Slightly wounded.
G.B. Ross........	First sergeant	G, Captain Burgwin.	First U.S. Dragoons.	Killed.
Brooks.............	Private...........	........do............	........do.................	Do.
Beebes.............	........do...........	........do............	........do.................	Do.
Levicy..............	........do...........	........do............	........do.................	Do.
Hansuker.........	........do...........	........do............	........do.................	Do.
Captain Burgwin	Captain..........	........do............	........do.................	Mortally wounded (since dead).
I. Vanroe.........	Sergeant........	........do............	........do.................	Severely wounded.
C. Ingleman.....	Corporal.......	........do............	........do.................	Do.
I.L. Linneman..	......do...........	........do............	........do.................	Do.
S. Blodget........	Private...........	........do............	........do.................	Do.
S.W. Crain.......	........do...........	........do............	........do.................	Do.
R. Deets...........	........do...........	........do............	........do.................	Do.
G.F. Sickenberg	........do...........	........do............	........do.................	Do.
I. Truax...........	........do...........	........do............	........do.................	Severely wounded (since dead).
Hagenbagh......	........do...........	........do............	........do.................	Severely wounded.
Anderson.........	........do...........	........do............	........do.................	Do.
Beach..............	........do...........	........do............	........do.................	Slightly wounded.
Hutton............	........do...........	........do............	........do.................	Do.
Hillerman........	........do...........	........do............	........do.................	Do.
Walker, 1st......	........do...........	........do............	........do.................	Do.
Schneider........	........do...........	........do............	........do.................	Severely wounded (since dead).
Shay................	........do...........	........do............	........do.................	Severely wounded.

AT PUEBLO DE TAOS, ON FEBRUARY 4, 1847.

Names	Rank	Company	Regiment and battalion	Remarks
Wounded-Cont.				
Near.................	......do...........	........do.............	........do...............	Do.
Bremen............	......do...........	I, Capt Burgwin.	........do...............	Do.
Biefeld.............	......do...........	B, Missouri Artillery.	Lieutenant Dyer's detachment.	Do.
Jod...................	......do...........	......do.............	........do...............	Do.
Kohn................	......do...........	......do.............	........do...............	Slightly wounded.
Hart.................	Sergeant........	Captain Angney	Infantry battalion	Killed.
Ferguson..........	......do...........	......do.............	........do...............	Badly wounded.
Aull.................	......do...........	......do.............	........do...............	Do.
Van Valkenberg	Lieutenant.....	B, Captain Angney.	........do...............	Mortally wounded (since dead).
Gold................	Private...........	Santa Fe Volunteers.	Captain St. Vrains	Severely wounded.
Mitchell...........	......do...........	......do.............	........do...............	Slightly wounded.

In addition to the foregoing, Captain Hendly was killed at the town of Mora on the 24th of January last, and on the same day three men were wounded at the same place.

APPENDIX D

A Description of New Mexico in 1846

The following is First Lieutenant William H. Emory's description of New Mexico as he found it in the fall of 1846. Emory was the senior topographical engineer in Colonel Stephen Watts Kearny's "Army of the West."

New Mexico contains, according to the last census, made a few years since, 100,000 inhabitants. It is divided into three departments—the northern, middle, and southeastern. These are again subdivided into counties, and the counties into townships. The lower or southern division is incomparably the richest, containing 48,000 inhabitants, many of whom are wealthy and in possession of farms, stock, and gold dust.

New Mexico, although its soil is barren, and its resources limited, unless the gold mines should, as is probable, be more extensively developed hereafter, and the culture of the grape enlarged, is, from its position, in a commercial and military aspect, an all-important military possession for the United States. The road from Santa Fé to Fort Leavenworth presents few obstacles for a railway, and, if it continues as good to the Pacific, will be one of the routes to be considered, over which the United States will pass immense quantities of merchandise into what may become, in time, the rich and populous States of Sonora, Durango, and Southern California.

As a military position, it is important and necessary. The mountain fastnesses have long been the retreating places of the warlike parties of Indians and robbers, who sally out to intercept our caravans moving over the different lines of travel to the Pacific.

The latitude of Santa Fé...is N. 35° 44' 06". The longitude ...brought by the chronometer from the meridian of Fort Leavenworth is 7*h*. 04*m*. 05*s*.5.

The place of observation was the court near the northeast corner of the public square....

The mean of all the barometric readings at Santa Fé indicates, as the height of this point above the sea, 6,846 feet, and the neighboring peaks to the north are many thousand feet higher.

Source: Emory, Lieut. Col. W.H., *Notes of a Military Reconnoissance, from Fort Leavenworth, in Missouri, to San Diego, in California, including part of the Arkansas, Del Norte, and Gila Rivers.* Thirtieth Congress, First Session, Executive Document No. 41. (Washington, D.C.: Wendell and Van Benthuysen, Printers, 1848), pp. 35-36.

APPENDIX E

A Description of
Taos and Vicinity

The following is a description of the town of Taos, the Taos Pueblo, and the surrounding area in early 1847, as related by Lieutenant W.G. Peck of the Topographical Engineers.

The name Taos, originally given to the region of country embracing the head waters of a river of the same name, has long since, by universal custom, been applied to the particular settlement of San Fernandez. This town is situated at the junction of the two principal forks of the "Rio de Taos," and 4 or 5 miles from the western base of the Rocky mountain range. Like most of the New Mexican towns it consists of a collection of mud houses, built around a miserable square or plaza. It contains a mixed population of 700 or 800 souls, and, besides being the capital of the northeastern department, possesses little to interest the traveller.

Three miles to the southeast is another town, of about equal pretensions, called "Rancho de Taos;" whilst at about the same distance to the northeast is the celebrated "Pueblo de Taos." This village, interesting in itself as a curius relic of the Aztecan age, is rendered still more so by the recent tragic scenes that have been enacted within its walls. One of the northern forks of the Taos river, on issuing from the mountains, forms a delightful nook, which the Indians early selected as a permanent residence. By gradual improvement, from year to year, it has finally become one of the most formidable of the artificial strongholds of New Mexico. On each side of the little mountain stream is one of those immense "adobe" structures, which rises by successive steps until an irregular pyramidal building, seven stories high, presents an almost impregnable tower. These, with the church and some few scattering houses, make up the village. The whole is surrounded by an adobe wall, strengthened in some places by rough palisades, the different parts so arranged, for mutual defence, as to have elicited much admiration for the skill of the untaught engineers....

Built of "adobes," a material almost impenetrable by shot, having no external entrance except through the roof, which must be reached by moveable ladders, each story smaller than the one below, irregular in its plan, and the whole judiciously pierced with loop-holes for defence, the combination presents a system of fortification peculiarly "sui generis."

These three towns constitute the principal settlements in the valley, though there are some scattering houses along the water courses. The valley may be eight or nine miles in length from east to west, and some seven or eight miles in width from north to south, embracing about sixty square miles. Only a small portion of this is under cultivation, or indeed ever can be, as no rain falls here except during the wet season. It is necessary to irrigate all the cultivated land, and the small supply of water fixes a limit, and that a very narrow one, to all the tillable land. In point of soil, the valley of Taos compares favorably with other portions of New Mexico; and though snow is to be seen in every month of the year, on the neighboring mountains, wheat and corn ripen very well on the plains. These last are the staple productions of the country; though beans, pumpkins, melons, and red pepper are raised to some extent. The hills are covered with very good grass, which furnishes subsistence to herds of cattle and horses, as well as to fine flocks of sheep and goats. In them lie the principal wealth of the inhabitants.

Taos is, by nature, almost isolated from the remainder of New Mexico. On the east rise the high peaks of the main Rocky mountain chain, whilst a spur of the same range puts out on the south quite to the banks of the Rio del Norte. On the north and west are the high bluffs which mark the beginning of the extensive "llanos," or table lands. A wagon road of some difficulty has been opened through the southern spur, which leads to Santa Fé, though the communication is usually kept up by the shorter mule road, over the highest point of the spur.

Source: Abert, Lieutenant J.W., *Report of the Secretary of War*, Thirtieth Congress, First Session, Executive Document No. 23 (Washington, D.C., 1848), pp. 40-42.

BIBLIOGRAPHY

Abert, J.W. *Report of Lieut. J.W. Abert, of his Examination of New Mexico in the Years 1846-'47*. Washington, D.C.: 30th Congress, 1st Session, 1848. Executive Document 23.

Adams, James Truslow, ed. *Atlas of American History*. New York: Charles Scribner's Sons, 1943.

Bannon, John Francis. *The Spanish Borderlands Frontier, 1513-1821*. New York: Holt, Rinehart and Winston, 1970.

Barry, Louise. *The Beginnings of the West*. Topeka: Kansas State Historical Society, 1972.

Bauer, K. Jack. *The Mexican War, 1846-1848*. New York: Macmillan Publishing Company, Inc., 1974.

Beachum, Larry M. *William Becknell—Father of the Santa Fe Trade*. El Paso: Texas Western Press, 1982.

Benton, Thomas Hart. *Thirty Years' View*. New York: D. Appleton and Company, 1854.

Bent's Old Fort. N.P.: The State Historical Society of Colorado, 1979.

Bezy, John V. and Sanchez, Joseph P., ed. *Pecos: Gateway to Pueblos and Plains, The Anthology*. Tucson: Southwest Parks & Monuments Association, 1988.

Bieber, Ralph P., ed. *Marching with the Army of the West 1846-1848*. Philadelphia: Porcupine Press, 1974.

Bolton, Herbert E. *The Spanish Borderlands*. New Haven: Yale University Press, 1921.

Brooks, N.C. *A Complete History of the Mexican War: Its Causes, Conduct, and Consequences*. Philadelphia: Grigg, Elliot & Company, 1849.

Brown, Dee. *The Westerners*. New York: Holt, Rinehart and Winston, 1974.

Brown, William E. *The Santa Fe Trail*. St. Louis: The Patrice Press, 1988.

Bryan, Howard. *Wildest of the Wild West: True Tales of a Frontier Town on the Santa Fe Trail*. Santa Fe: Clear Light Publishers, 1988.

Carson, Phil. "The Taos Uprising of 1847," in *True West Magazine*. Stillwater, Oklahoma: Western Publications, June, 1986.

Cheetham, Francis T. "The First Term of the American Court in Taos, New Mexico," in *New Mexico Historical Review*. Santa Fe: New Mexico Historical Society, Vol. 1, No. 1, January, 1926.

Conard, Howard Louis. *"Uncle Dick" Wootton*. Chicago: W.E. Dibble & Company, 1890.

Cooke, Philip St. George. *The Conquest of New Mexico and California*. Chicago: The Rio Grande Press, Inc., 1964.

Crutchfield, James A. *It Happened in Colorado*. Helena, Montana: Falcon Press, 1993.

_____. "Marching with the Army of the West," in *Black Powder Annual*. Union City, Tennessee: Dixie Gun Works, Inc., 1991.

_____. *Tennesseans at War*. Nashville: Rutledge Hill Press, 1987.

_____. *The Santa Fe Trail*. Unpublished Manuscript.

_____. "The Taos Revolt of 1847," in *Muzzle Blasts Magazine*. Friendship, Indiana: The National Muzzle Loading Rifle Association, January, 1986.

_____. "When all Hell Broke Loose in Taos," in *Black Powder Annual*. Union City, Tennessee: Dixie Gun Works, 1990.

Davis, Louise Littleton. *Frontier Tales of Tennessee*. New Orleans: Pelican Publishing Company, 1976.

Day, A. Grove. *Coronado's Quest*. Berkeley: University of California Press, 1964.

Delgado, Deane G., compiler. *Historical Markers of New Mexico*. Santa Fe: Ancient City Press, 1990.

De Voto, Bernard. *The Year of Decision: 1846*. New York: Book-of-the-Month Club, Inc., 1984.

Edwards, Frank S. *A Campaign in New Mexico*. N.P.: Readex Microprint Corporation, 1966.

Emory, W.H. *Notes of a Military Reconnoissance, from Fort Leavenworth, in Missouri, to San Diego, in California, including part of the Arkansas, Del Norte, and Gila Rivers*. Washington, D.C.: 30th Congress, 1st Session, 1848. Executive Document 41.

Frost, J. *The Mexican War and Its Warriors*. New Haven: H. Mansfield, 1850.

Gabriel, Ralph Henry. *The Lure of the Frontier*. New Haven: Yale University Press, 1929.

Galbraith, Den. *Turbulent Taos*. Santa Fe: Sunstone Press, 1983.

Galvin, John, ed. *Western America in 1846-1847: The Original Travel Diary of Lieutenant J.W. Abert*. San Francisco: John Howell-Books, 1966.

Garrard, Lewis H. *Wah-To-Yah and the Taos Trail*. Norman: University of Oklahoma Press, 1955.

Gone West. St. Louis: The Jefferson National Expansion Historical Association, Winter, 1984.

Gregg, Josiah. *Commerce of the Prairies, or the Journal of a Santa Fe Trader, during Eight Expeditions across the Great Western Prairies, and a Residence of Nearly Nine Years in Northern Mexico*. New York: Henry G. Langley, 1844.

_____. *Commerce of the Prairies*. Edited by Max L. Moorhead. Norman: University of Oklahoma Press, 1954.

Heitman, Francis B. *Historical Register and Dictionary of the United States Army*. Washington, D.C.: Government Printing Office, 1903.

Herr, John K. and Wallace, Edward S. *The Story of the U.S. Cavalry*. New York: Bonanza Books, 1984.

Horgan, Paul. *Great River: The Rio Grande in North American History*. New York: Rinehart & Company, Inc., 1954.

_____. *Under the Sangre de Christo*. Flagstaff, Arizona: Northland Press, 1985.

Hughes, John T. *Doniphan's Expedition; Containing an Account of the Conquest of New Mexico*. Cincinnati: J.A. & U.P. James, 1850.

Inaugural Addresses of the Presidents of the United States. Washington, D.C.: 101st Congress, 1st Session, 1989. Senate Document 101-10.

Insurrection Against the Military Government in New Mexico and California, 1847 and 1848. Washington, D.C.: 56th Congress, 1st Session, 1900. Senate Document 442.

James, Marquis. *The Life of Andrew Jackson*. Indianapolis: The Bobbs-Merrill Company, 1938.

_____. *The Raven*. Indianapolis: The Bobbs-Merrill Company, 1929.

James, General Thomas. *Three Years among the Indians and Mexicans*. New York: The Citidel Press, 1966.

Jenkins, John S. *The Life of James Knox Polk, Late President of the United States*. Auburn, New York: James M. Alden, 1850.

Kendall, George Wilkins. *Narrative of the Texan Santa Fé Expedition*. New York: Harper and Brothers, 1844.

Kessell, John L. *Kiva, Cross, and Crown*. Washington, D.C.: National Park Service, 1979.

Lamar, Howard R., ed. *The Reader's Encyclopedia of the American West*. New York: Harper & Row, Publishers, 1977.

Lavender, David. *Bent's Fort*. Garden City, New York: Doubleday & Company, Inc., 1954.

Long, Jeff. *Duel of Eagles*. New York: William Morrow and Company, Inc., 1990.

Loomis, Noel M. and Nasatir, Abraham P. *Pedro Vial and the Roads to Santa Fe*. Norman: University of Oklahoma Press, 1967.

Loomis, Noel M. *The Texan-Santa Fe Pioneers*. Norman: University of Oklahoma Press, 1958.

Love, Marian F. "The Demise of Turley's Mill," in *The Santa Fean Magazine*. Santa Fe, 1986.

Loyola, Sister Mary. "The American Occupation of New Mexico, 1821-1852," in *New Mexico Historical Review*. Santa Fe: The New Mexico Historical Society, Vol. 14, No. 3, July, 1939.

Magoffin, Susan Shelby. *Down the Santa Fe Trail and Into Mexico*. Edited by Stella M. Drumm. Lincoln: University of Nebraska Press, 1982.

McNierney, Michael, ed. *Taos 1847: The Revolt in Contemporary Accounts*. Boulder, Colorado: Johnson Publishing Company, 1980.

Meriwether, David. *My Life in the Mountains and on the Plains*. Norman: University of Oklahoma Press, 1965.

Mumey, Nolie, ed. *Laws of the Territory of New Mexico*. Denver: Nolie Mumey, 1970.

_____. *Old Forts and Trading Posts of the West*. Denver: Artcraft Press, 1956.

Myers, John Myers. *The Deaths of the Bravos*. Boston: Little, Brown and Company, 1962.

Nevin, David. *The Mexican War*. Alexandria, Virginia: Time-Life Books, 1978.

_____. *The Texans*. Alexandria, Virginia: Time-Life Books, 1975.

Nevins, Allan, ed. *Polk, The Diary of a President*. New York: Longmans, Green and Company, 1952.

_____, ed. *The Diary of Philip Hone 1828-1851*. New York: Dodd, Mead and Company, 1927.

Noble, David Grant. "Pecos Pueblo, December 31, 1590," in *Exploration*. Santa Fe: School of American Research, 1981.

_____. *Santa Fe—History of an Ancient City*. Santa Fe: School of American Research, 1989.

Oglesby, Richard Edward. *Manuel Lisa and the Opening of the Missouri Fur Trade*. Norman: University of Oklahoma Press, 1963.

Pearce, T.M., ed. *New Mexico Place Names: A Geographical Dictionary*. Albuquerque: University of New Mexico Press, 1965.

Polk, James K. *Occupation of Mexican Territory*. Message from the President of the United States. 29th Congress, 2d Session, 1846. Executive Document 19.

Prince, L. Bradford. *Old Fort Marcy*. Santa Fe: New Mexican Printing Company, 1912.

Quaife, Milo Milton, ed. *Kit Carson's Autobiography*. Lincoln: University of Nebraska Press, 1966.

Remini, Robert V. *Andrew Jackson and the Course of American Democracy*. New York: Harper & Row, Publishers, Volumes 2 & 3, 1981 & 1984.

Rittenhouse, Jack D. *The Santa Fe Trail: A Historical Bibliography*. Albuquerque: Jack D. Rittenhouse, 1986.

Ruxton, George Frederick. *Life in the Far West*, edited by Leroy R. Hafen. Norman: University of Oklahoma Press, 1951.

Schubert, Frank N. *Vanguard of Expansion: Army Engineers in the Trans-Mississippi West, 1819-1879*. Washington, D.C.: Historical Division, Office of Administrative Services, Office of the Chief of Engineers, United States Army, n.d.

Sunder, John E. *Matt Field on the Santa Fe Trail*. Norman: University of Oklahoma Press, 1960.

Terrell, John Upton. *American Indian Almanac*. New York: The World Publishing Company, 1971.

The Spanish West. Alexandria, Virginia: Time-Life Books, 1976.

Thrapp Dan L. *Encyclopedia of Frontier Biography*. Glendale, California: The Arthur H. Clark Company, 1988.

Traas, Adrian George. *From the Golden Gate to Mexico City: The U.S. Topographical Engineers in the Mexican War, 1846-1848*. Washington, D.C.: Office of History, Corps of Engineers, United States Army, 1993.

Turner, Don. *The Massacre of Gov. Bent*. Amarillo: Humbug Gulch Press, 1969.

Twitchell, Ralph Emerson. *The History of the Military Occupation of the Territory of New Mexico from 1846 to 1851*. Denver: The Smith-Brooks Company, Publishers, 1909.

_____. *The Story of the Conquest of Santa Fe, New Mexico, and The Building of Old Fort Marcy, A.D. 1846*. Santa Fe: Historical Society of New Mexico, n.d.

Urwin, Gregory J.W. *The United States Cavalry: An Illustrated History*. Poole, Dorset, U.K.: Blandford Press, 1983.

Utley, Robert M. *Frontiersmen in Blue*. Lincoln: University of Nebraska Press, 1981.

Walter, Paul A.F. "First Civil Governor of New Mexico," in *The New Mexico Historical Review*. Santa Fe: The New Mexico Historical Society, Vol. 8, No. 2, April, 1933.

Weber, David J. *The Mexican Frontier 1821-1846*. Albuquerque: University of New Mexico Press, 1982.

_____. *The Spanish Frontier in America*. New Haven: Yale University Press, 1992.

_____. *The Taos Trappers*. Norman: University of Oklahoma Press, 1971.

Weems, John Edward. *Men Without Countries*. Boston: Houghton Mifflin Company, 1969.

_____. *To Conquer a Peace*. College Station, Texas: Texas A&M University, 1988.

Wislizenus, A. *Memoir of A Tour to Northern Mexico, Connected With Col. Doniphan's Expedition*. Washington, D.C.: 30th Congress, 1st Session, 1848. Senate Miscellaneous Document 26.

Wood, William and Gabriel, Ralph Henry. *The Winning of Freedom*. New Haven: Yale University Press, 1927.

Index

Since the vast majority of the story told in this book occurred in New Mexico, specifically in the towns of Santa Fe and Taos, no effort has been made to index entries for those three headings.